Carrickfergus

The Story of the Castle & Walled Town

Ruairí Ó Baoill

Applications for reproduction should be made in writing to The Stationery Office Ltd, St Crispins, Duke Street, Norwich NR3 1PD.

The information contained in this publication is believed to be correct at the time of manufacture. Whilst care has been taken to ensure that the information is accurate, the publisher can accept no responsibility for any errors or omissions or for changes to the details given.

A CIP catalogue record for this book is available from the British Library.
A Library of Congress CIP catalogue record has been applied for.

First published 2008

ISBN 978-0-337-08956-5

Printed in Northern Ireland by Graham & Heslip, Belfast, Co. Antrim

Contents

Acknowledgements

The author would like to thank the following persons:

Claire Foley, Dr Brian Williams, Ken Neill, Dr John O'Keeffe and Paul Logue, Northern Ireland Environment Agency – Built Heritage (NIEA) who were all involved in various ways in commissioning this book and facilitating its publication.

Drs Colm Donnelly and Philip Macdonald, Centre for Archaeological Fieldwork, School of Geography, Archaeology and Palaeoecology, Queen's University Belfast (CAF) and Dr Brian Scott for reading over various drafts or sections of the book and making useful suggestions for its improvement.

Gail Pollock, Tony Corey and Terence Reeves-Smyth (NIEA) and Dr. Eileen Murphy, School of Geography, Archaeology and Palaeoecology, Queen's University Belfast, who provided the photographic images used in the book.

Naomi Carver (CAF), Mark Mulholland, Eoin Lennon and Patricia Ó Baoill who created the new maps, plans and annotated images used in the book.

Dr. Chris Lynn for information on recent excavations in Carrickfergus.

Maureen McCorry for material from an unpublished manuscript on the geology of Carrickfergus prepared for the NIEA.

Sheelagh Hughes of Editorial Solutions who did the initial proofing of the book, to Roisin McAuley and Bryan McCann of Leslie Stannage Design for the graphic layout and to Marie Maguire and her colleagues at TSO Ireland for managing the publication process.

Julitta Clancy for compiling the index for the book.

In Carrickfergus:
Fr. Seán Dillon, St. Nicholas' Church, Minorca Place for allowing access to the O'Neill Chalice.
Ted McAuley (Secretary) and the Vestry of St. Nicholas' Church, Lancasterian Street, for facilitating photography within the Church.
Helen Rankin for continued interest and support.

Finally, the author would like to put on record his special debt of gratitude to Gail Pollock, NIEA. She steered the book from is inception to publication and without her continued commitment it would never have been produced.

About the Author

Ruairí Ó Baoill is a specialist in Medieval and Post-Medieval archaeology. After graduating from Queen's University Belfast in 1985 with a Joint Honours degree in Archaeology and Ancient History he worked within commercial-sector archaeology on a wide range of urban excavations in Dublin, Limerick, Carrickfergus and Sligo. He directed his first excavation in 1991 and since that time has been involved in dozens of projects, including large-scale projects with multiple excavations.

From 1998 to 2002 Ruairí was a member of the Environmental Heritage Service (EHS): Built Heritage's Archaeological Excavation Unit. Since August 2005 he has been working with the Centre for Archaeological Fieldwork, School of Geography, Archaeology and Palaeoecology, Queen's University Belfast in bringing to publication level his State-funded excavations. He is also currently project managing to publication the final report on his major programme of 12 excavations at Carrickfergus. He directed this programme on behalf of EHS: Built Heritage from 1991 to 1995 and which will be the largest urban excavation report ever to be produced in Northern Ireland.

Ruairí has taught a variety of courses in archaeology to adult learners; he was a part-time lecturer in archaeology at the Belfast Institute from 1994 to 1997, and he was course co-coordinator of the Certificate Course in Archaeology with the Institute of Continuing Education at Queen's University Belfast from 1998 to 1999. He has served on the Board of the Institute of Archaeologists of Ireland (IAI) and was a founder member and former Chair of the Irish Post-Medieval Archaeology Group (IPMAG).

For Patricia and Conal Óg

1. Introduction

The modern visitor to Carrickfergus will experience a town that is very different to the one that existed for most of its long history. The essential and symbiotic relationship that existed for centuries between the town and the castle was severed by the construction of a major road, the Marine Highway (now the Causeway Coastal Route), in the late 1960s. As a result, the altered townscape can sometimes be difficult to understand. This book will unravel the mysteries of Carrickfergus and help visitors understand why, for so long, it was the most important town in Ulster.

Carrickfergus has been a town for over 800 years. It is a living entity, created and used by the people who lived there, folk that in this book we will bring to life. Over eight centuries, layers of history have accumulated within the town. The purpose of this book is to examine these layers, so that a person visiting the modern town can see the key elements from the significant phases in its history. This is one of the most excavated towns in Ulster, and the day-to-day lives of its people over many centuries can be reconstructed by archaeologists from the objects that the townsfolk lost or discarded and by examination of the buildings in which they lived. A number of major monuments survive in the town — the castle, St Nicholas' Church and the town walls. All of these represent important stages in the history and development of the town, and are explored in separate sections in this book.

The story of Carrickfergus is exciting — full of sieges by English, Scottish and Irish kings and lords, attacks by American revolutionaries and French troops. However, towns do not exist in a vacuum. They are located in a host landscape that influences how the town

John de Courcy

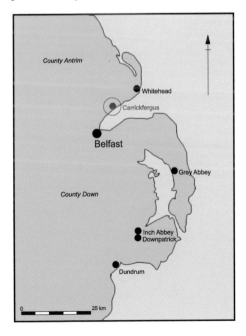

Location map of Carrickfergus

1

Photograph of Carrickfergus Castle and town, circa 1950. Note the proximity of town buildings to the entrance to the fortification. This would have been the situation for most of the 800-year history of Carrickfergus

develops. Therefore, before we tell the story of Carrickfergus, we must describe the geography, geology and archaeological background of the area to show how these influenced the origins and development of the town.

2. The Geographical, Geological and Archaeological Background to Carrickfergus Town and Castle

Geography

Carrickfergus is located on the southern coast of County Antrim, looking out on Belfast Lough. A coastal plain, overlooked by the southern limit of the Antrim basalts and up to four kilometres in width, runs inland from the town and the north-western shore of the lough. Close by, the mountains take the form of a moderately steep scarp-face on hills that rise to some 200 metres above sea level (but at Belfast are very high and steep). The coastal plain to the west is dominated by a flat-topped summit known as 'The Knockagh', 300 metres above sea level. To the east of this summit and north of the town, the coastal plain is only about three kilometres wide. Therefore, although passage along inland routes was possible, it could also have been fraught with danger and the possibility of being attacked. It would have been safer to travel along this stretch of Belfast Lough by boat.

Geology

The geology of the area around Carrickfergus is dominated by a sequence of underformed and relatively horizontal sedimentary and igneous rocks, ranging in age from Triassic (208–245 million years old) to Tertiary (from 1 million to over 66 million years old). The oldest rocks — Triassic Keuper marls — outcrop on the shore. The castle is located on a Tertiary olivine gabbro intrusion, and a number of contemporary basaltic dykes, trending north-west/south-east, crop out along the shore.

The area around Carrickfergus is covered in boulder clay weathered from fluvio-glacial deposits, except for the sand and gravel of the raised (and modern) beach and alluvial deposits of river beds. Archaeological excavations have shown that the Keuper marls were exploited by the people of Carrickfergus from the Medieval Period onwards. It was used for pottery-making, as well as for export throughout Ireland and Britain as pipe-clay from the 17th century onwards, and for brick-making from at least the 19th century.

Most of the building stone used in the fabric of the castle and town walls was local basalt, but dressed sandstone was brought from places as far away as Cushendun on the Antrim coast, and Cultra in County Down, while limestone was quarried from nearby Whitehead.

Earlier Archaeological Sites in the Environs of Carrickfergus

The Ordnance Survey 6" map of 1837 depicts an Early Christian rath

Photograph of the castle showing the rocky outcrop on which it was built

Early Christian rath

(farmstead), which no longer exists, in the environs of Shaftsbury Park, but there does not appear to have been any nucleated settlement in the environs of the town prior to the arrival of the Anglo-Normans in the late 1170s. However, there is a number of Early Christian and possibly prehistoric sites in the wider hinterland, implying that there was quite intensive dispersed settlement in the area prior to the founding of the town.

The information on all these sites is housed in the Northern Ireland Sites and Monuments Record (NISMR) in the Northern Ireland Environment Agency (NIEA), Waterman House, Hill Street, Belfast. There are records of 14,500 archaeological sites and historic monuments. Every archaeological site and monument in Northern Ireland has a dedicated number, file and is marked on the relevant Ordnance Survey map for its particular county. So a site with the NISMR number Antrim 052:146 means that the site can be located on sheet 52 of the Ordnance Survey maps of County Antrim and is marked on this map with the specific number 146. Antrim 052: 146 is also the number of the file relating to the site.

Instead of having townland names, the areas around Carrickfergus are known as North-East Division, Middle Division, West Division and the Commons. These divisions are much larger than townlands, the usual division of land in Ireland. They relate to an arrangement agreed between Carrickfergus corporation and the Crown at the end of the 16th century for freemen of the town to receive portions of land around the town. These land division names have remained to this day.

Archaeological sites in immediate vicinity of Carrickfergus include a Bronze Age *fulachta fiadh*, or cooking place, and two barrows in Middle Division (NISMR Antrim 052:146, 052:011 and 052:012); a possible cairn in the Commons (NISMR Antrim 052:069); enclosures in both Middle Division and East Central Ward (NISMR Antrim 052:023 and 052:064); circular enclosures in Middle Division (NISMR Antrim 052:108 and 052:109); an enclosure and souterrain in West Division (NISMR Antrim 052:034); a souterrain in West Division (NISMR Antrim 052:033) and raths in North-East Division (NISMR Antrim 052:129 and 052:135), Middle Division (NISMR Antrim 052:020, 052:126 and 052:085), West Division (NISMR 052:029 and 052:032 and Carrickfergus West Ward (NISMR Antrim 052:030).

The name Carrickfergus derives from the Irish word for the rock on which the castle was to be built; *Carraig Fheargas* or the Rock of Fergus. Irish legend has it that a king of Dalriada (north-eastern Ireland and south-western Scotland), Fergus Mór Mac Eirc, drowned at the rock while seeking a medicinal cure for his leprosy from the natural well that was located on the rock and so gave his name to the place.

3. Anglo-Norman Carrickfergus

John de Courcy

In 1177, eight years after the Anglo-Norman invasion of south-eastern Ireland, John de Courcy led an army of 22 knights and 300 foot soldiers from Dublin into Ulster. De Courcy was the younger son of a Somerset knight and in 1176, when he first came to Ireland with William Fitz Audelin, deputy of the English King Henry II, he was based in Dublin as part of the city garrison. Although sanctioned by Henry, the invasion of Ulster was a de Courcy-led freelance operation to capture as much land from the Irish as was possible.

When de Courcy arrived at Carrickfergus in the late 1170s he

Anglo-Norman warrior

The castle under construction

Cultra stone

Affreca

King John

found that the location suited him as a principal base of operations, and started the construction of a castle on a promontory that projects out from the northern shore of Belfast Lough. The town of Carrickfergus grew up in the shadow of its castle. The location allowed de Courcy to:

(a) guard access to Belfast Lough;
(b) guard the route through the coastal plain through the hills to north Antrim;
(c) make use of the natural harbour west of the castle;
(d) ensure secure communications with his allies in England and the Isle of Man (the daughter of whose king, de Courcy was to marry).

The first phase of construction of Carrickfergus Castle – principally the keep and inner ward –began soon after de Courcy's arrival in Ulster. The basic material used in the construction was local basalt rubble, but for fine dressed work in the earlier buildings red sandstone and Cultra limestone were used. The efforts of the Irish lords in Ulster to wipe out the Anglo-Norman settlement before it could take hold meant that a speedy construction of a fortified base was a priority. Excavations within the castle suggest that both the lower courses of the inner ward defensive wall and the keep were built between 1177 and 1181. It seems that shortly after this date an accommodation was reached between the Anglo-Normans and the Irish, and de Courcy was left free to continue the building work under less stressful conditions than when he first arrived.

In 1185, King Henry II made de Courcy Judiciar (Chief Official) of Ireland. Based far away from the centre of Norman administration at Dublin, the lands de Courcy controlled were ruled in a semi-independent manner. He

minted his own coins at both Carrickfergus and Downpatrick, and is described in contemporary documents as Princeps Ulidiae – Prince of Ulster – although this was never an official title conferred by the Crown.

The area of Ulster controlled by the Anglo-Normans during the Medieval Period corresponded roughly with the eastern coastal areas of (modern) Counties Antrim and Down. Between the late 1170s and his downfall in 1205, de Courcy and his wife Affreca founded several monastic houses in the region, including Inch Abbey and Grey Abbey. Another formidable castle at Dundrum, County Down, was constructed to guard the southern portion of the area under Anglo-Norman control.

Only two monuments from Anglo-Norman Carrickfergus survive today: the castle and St Nicholas' Church. The history and development of the castle will be dealt with later, in chapter 5, and that of St Nicholas' Church in chapter 8. Here we need only note that St Nicholas' Church was probably founded soon after John de Courcy's arrival at Carrickfergus, along with a Premonstratensian abbey (now vanished), with Canons from Dryburgh Abbey in Berwickshire.

Thus, Carrickfergus was developed both as an important military outpost and an ecclesiastical centre. The site of the Premonstratensian abbey has been located at Woodburn (NISMR Antrim 052:031), but structural evidence of the actual church itself has not been uncovered. The site of another Medieval foundation, St Brides' [Bridget's] Hospital and Well, is also thought to be located in North-East Division, Carrickfergus (NISMR Antrim 052:058). Recent excavations at the presumed location uncovered the skeletons of 12 adults, juveniles and infants.

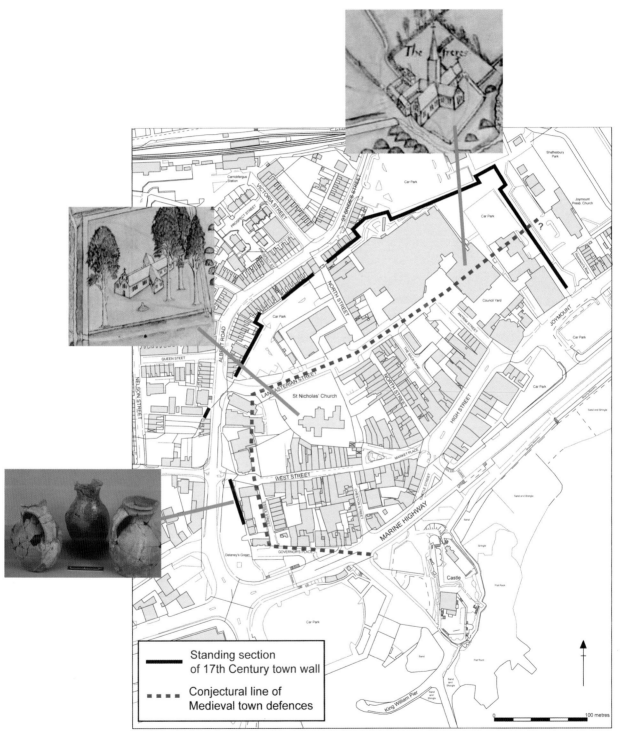

Map showing the layout of Anglo-Norman Carrickfergus, the location of the town defences, St Nicholas' Church, the Franciscan Friary (from the 1560 map) and the pottery kiln

7

Battering ram

Fearing that John de Courcy was creating an entirely independent kingdom in Ulster, King John, who acceded to the English throne in 1199, encouraged Hugh de Lacy, another powerful Anglo-Norman knight who held lands in County Meath, to take control from him. In the fighting that took place between them, de Lacy decisively defeated de Courcy forcing him into exile for a short while in 1205. However, anxious to regain his lands, de Courcy continued fighting, unsuccessfully invading Ulster from the Isle of Man.

Interestingly, Carrickfergus does not get mentioned in the written accounts of this struggle. After his final defeat de Courcy again went into exile and, although he appears to have been in King John's army in Ireland in 1210, he died in obscurity in 1219 having failed to take back his Ulster lands.

Hugh de Lacy

Hugh de Lacy came to Ireland in 1195, the second son of Hugh de Lacy of Herefordshire, who accompanied Henry II on his expedition to Ireland in 1171. Hugh the elder was granted the Irish Kingdom of Mide (Meath) and built the principal castle of the de Lacys at Trim, making it one of the strongest castles in Ireland. King John used Hugh the younger to destroy his former ally John de Courcy and, in reward, made him the first Earl of Ulster.

As the resident lord in Ulster, Hugh de Lacy acquired lands that included Carrickfergus and its castle. But soon he, like de Courcy before him, begain to act in a semi-autonomous manner. This again incurred the wrath of King John who came to Ulster in person in 1210 to take control of the earldom. Carrickfergus Castle was put under siege, and Hugh de Lacy expelled. The castle was transferred into the custody of the Crown which is how it remained until 1226. During this period, the middle ward was constructed.

As regards the Medieval town, it is clear that within a few short decades a settlement, including religious houses, had grown up around the castle. Historical documents refer in 1221 to burgesses (citizens or freemen of a borough) and in 1226 Carrickfergus was described as a 'vill' (town).

In 1223 Hugh de Lacy, still in exile, invaded Ireland and put Carrickfergus under siege in an attempt to regain his lands. Things did not go well for him and he was forced to surrender in 1224. Despite this, in 1226 he was regranted the earldom and lands of Ulster by Henry III, now king, including the castle at Carrickfergus. During the remainder of his lordship, until his death in about 1242, he constructed the outer ward of the castle, including the gatehouse, so that the castle finally covered the whole of the promontory on which it stood.

Because so few Medieval buildings have survived, the early history of

Siege engine

Carrickfergus is unclear. We are reliant on both map evidence and the discoveries from archaeological excavations to try to fill in the blanks. Unfortunately, the earliest map of Carrickfergus dates to *circa* 1560, almost 400 years after the castle and town were established. The 1560 map, the earliest of any town in Ulster, depicts the castle and the principal buildings within the town, and along with other 16th-century maps will be discussed in detail in chapter 6.

From the map and archaeological evidence, it appears that the Medieval town of Carrickfergus developed quickly. We do not have any records of the population of the town at this time, but it was probably in the low hundreds. The principal early streets were Cheston Street and Castle Street, running off from the outworks close to the castle entrance. The thoroughfare that we now know as High Street probably only evolved when the Franciscan Friary was built at the other end of the historic town core in the 1230s.

The Franciscan Friary

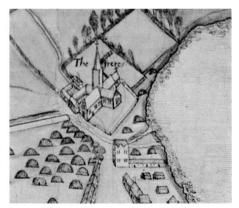

The Franciscan Friary from the 1560 map

The Franciscan Friary, also known as the Church of St Francis, was founded by Hugh de Lacy *circa* 1232 on the site where the present town hall and library

stand. In the Medieval Period, the friary stood just outside the eastern limits of the town. It seems to have had a mill within its building complex, and this is described in both the written sources and portrayed on the 1560 map, the only representation of the friary. Hugh de Lacy was buried here as well as members of the Clandeboye O'Neill dynasty. In the Late-Medieval Period the Clandeboye O'Neills were the main patrons of the church here. The friary was finally suppressed during the Reformation in Ireland in the mid-16th century and was later converted into a fortified storehouse known as the 'pallace'. Archaeological excavations carried out by Tom Delaney in the mid-1970s uncovered fragments of the friary walls and 68 skeletons, some of women and children, from the Medieval cemetery associated with it. Amongst the many artefacts recovered were fragments of painted window glass and decorated Medieval floor tiles, a glimpse of the friary's former splendour. More recent excavations by Moira O'Rourke also uncovered skeletons in the vicinity of the friary.

Carrickfergus after de Lacy

After Hugh de Lacy's death, the earldom once again reverted to the Crown. There are references to a mint being established in 1252, a privilege that shows the important status of the town, and there is another reference to burgesses in 1260. In 1265 the earldom passed to Walter de Burgh and the town seems to have prospered. There are references in 1274 to the mayor and commonality. However, there are no references to the properties or houses of ordinary townspeople before the 16th century. The location of Carrickfergus, surrounded by hostile Irish and Scots Gaelic territories on all sides meant that the settlement was, from its earliest days, in constant threat of

Silver coin minted at Carrickfergus

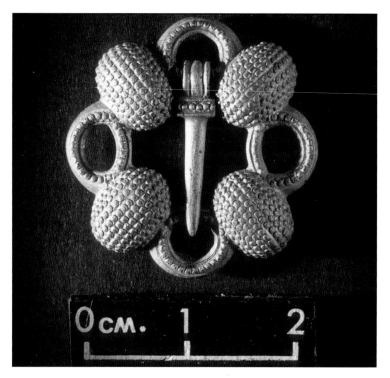

Early 13th-century gilded brooch

Medieval brooch

Medieval ring

onwards is uncertain, and the exact line of the eastern side of the Medieval town has yet to be found.

The fortifications consisted of an earthen bank supported by a palisade, inside a ditch approximately four metres wide. A 60-metre stretch of these defences was uncovered running through Joymount in the east of the town during excavations in the 1970s. In 1991–92, a shorter length of the 13th-century defences was archaeologically investigated at Essex Street in the west of the town. Excavations also uncovered a drawbridge pit that lay across the Essex Street defensive ditch, predating the nearby Irish Gate. Despite the constant threat of attack from the Irish and Scots during the Medieval Period, finds from archaeological excavations have revealed that Carrickfergus was prosperous for much of the time.

Evidence of Activities in and around the Town

Because of the risk of fire to the wooden buildings of the town, industrial activities were carried on outside the town boundaries.

There were potters from Chester operating in the town, and an excavation in 1979 uncovered one of their kilns, which was dated to the

attack. The Scots of the Glens burnt the town in 1274, but the castle was not damaged. The town recovered and was again described in 1285 as a 'vill'.

The Town Defences

Archaeological excavations carried out within the town have uncovered evidence of the defences that surrounded Carrickfergus during the Medieval Period, and the area enclosed has been estimated at approximately six to seven hectares. The line of the defences has been tracked running from the castle, up Essex Street (the western limit of the Medieval town) and turning east along Lancasterian Street (the northern limit of the Medieval town). In fact, it is very probable that the line of Lancasterian Street – a street not illustrated on maps until the late 16th century – represents the line of the defences at this point of the town. Although the defences were uncovered at Joymount, their course from this point

The Medieval pottery kiln during excavation in 1979. The pots are clearly visible within the chamber

Some of the reconstructed Medieval pots from the Carrickfergus kiln

Motte and bailey

first half of the 13th century, close to the Irish Gate.

High-status pottery from Bristol and various northern French towns was also being imported into the town. Sherds of Medieval Ulster coarse pottery, the unglazed ceramic used by the Irish in the areas outside Carrickfergus, have also been found in many excavations in the town. This suggests that, despite episodes of war between them, there was also plenty of interaction and trade between the Anglo-Normans and the Irish throughout the Medieval Period. The 'beehive' houses portrayed in the 16th-century maps (discussed in chapter six) also suggest that some Irish people may have been permitted to live in the town.

During the Medieval Period, the hinterland outside the town was used to provide the town with grain and other produce. Some of the monuments of the period survive to this day, although none has been archaeologically investigated to date. These include Duncrue Fort, consisting of a motte and an unusual arrangement of two baileys (NISMR Antrim 052:014); the nearby Killyann Church and graveyard (NISMR Antrim 052:016); and Dunrock rectangular enclosure and fortification (NISMR Antrim 052:015); all in Middle Division townland. Two possible ecclesiastical sites at Carnrawsy in Middle Division (NISMR Antrim 052:019) and Friar's Glen/Tobergal in West Division (NISMR Antrim 052:042) may also be of

Medieval date. Along with these known sites, many of the land divisions are of Medieval origin, though some were reorganised in the later 16th century. It is hoped that a detailed study of the sites and landscape that make up the hinterland around Carrickfergus will be undertaken in the near future which will help us understand how the landscape was organised around the town.

Excavations carried out from 1991–95 have also revealed aspects of the darker side of life in a frontier town in Medieval Ireland. One fifth of all dog bones recovered from these excavations displayed clear evidence of cut or chop marks (with some Post-Medieval animals also displaying the marks). Their presence on animal bone is a sure sign that a carcass was processed for food or as materials for human use. This processing involved four principal activities: skinning, dismemberment, meat removal and tool manufacture. The marks made during each of these procedures are distinct, and it is possible to reconstruct the activities that were responsible for the creation of most of them. Analysis by Dr Eileen Murphy indicates that the majority of the cut marks present on the Carrickfergus dog

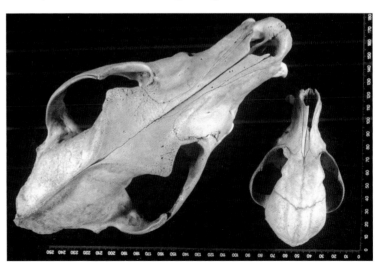

Butchered dog skulls

bones were related to the dismemberment and butchering of the carcasses. Some, however, were clearly the result of skinning. The butchers were not selective about which animals fell under the blade, with the young and the old, and the large and the small all suffering the same fate. Indeed, one pit contained the butchered remains of a group of puppies of less than five months old. The breakage patterns of the bones (for marrow extraction), the evidence of burning (indicative of cooking) and the location and presence of cut marks all indicate that the dogs were exploited both for their flesh and for their skins.

Carrickfergus experienced siege and attack throughout the Medieval Period, and it is possible that the high concentration of butchered dog bones relates to one or more episodes of warfare, where the population was reduced to eating animals in the town in order to survive. Alternatively, dogs may have been economically exploited for their meat and skins. After fish, hides are considered to have formed the main staple export from Ireland during the Late- Medieval Period. While there are no specific references to the export of dog skins from Carrickfergus, the documentary sources suggest that there was a considerable demand for hides for export. It is quite possible that dog skins were also being traded from this Irish port during the Medieval Period.

Edward Bruce Comes to Carrickfergus

As an extension of the wars between Scotland (ruled by King Robert the Bruce) and England (now ruled by King Edward I) a Scottish army invaded Ireland in 1315, led by Edward Bruce, the brother of the Scottish king. Many of the Ulster Irish chiefs, seeing an

opportunity to destroy the Anglo-Norman earldom, allied themselves to Bruce, and the English army sent to oppose him was defeated at the battle of Connor in County Antrim. The English retreated to Carrickfergus and Bruce with his Irish allies followed. The town was taken quickly and the castle put under siege. It is a testament to the strength of the fortifications that the garrison held out for a year. It is reported that in the end they were driven by starvation to eating some of their Scottish prisoners before surrendering in September 1316. After the surrender, Carrickfergus remained Edward Bruce's base in Ireland until his death in October 1318 in the battle at Faughart, near Dundalk, in County Louth.

The Decline of the Anglo-Norman Earldom of Ulster

The Anglo-Norman earldom of Ulster went into decline with the murder of

Tomb of Cooey-na-Gall O'Cahan at Dungiven Priory with Galloglas warriors shown below

William de Burgh, Earl of Ulster, in 1333. Henceforth, the area was governed by agents for the Sovereign, and there was never again a resident earl to make or direct policy for the earldom. Despite this, in 1334 Carrickfergus was referred to as a 'borough town', an indication of its importance. With the murder of the Earl came the rise to prominence of a branch of the Tyrone O'Neills known as the Clandeboye O'Neills. They came to control much of southern Antrim and northern Down and the situation of Carrickfergus became more precarious. The fact that Gaelic territory had encroached on the original area of the earldom meant that Carrickfergus was dependent for survival on supplies – both of men and provisions such as corn, wheat, oats and coal – arriving by sea from other Anglo-Norman-controlled areas along the eastern coast of Ireland, such as Drogheda. For many of the succeeding centuries it was the only major port in Ulster held for the Crown.

4. A Walk Through Anglo-Norman Carrickfergus

The first thing that anyone approaching the town of Carrickfergus in the Medieval Period, from any direction on land or sea, would have seen, even while still distant, would have been the silhouette of Carrickfergus Castle. As they got closer to the town, they would have been overwhelmed by this magnificent and overpowering stone fortification sitting dramatically atop a plateau of rock and jutting out into the sea.

The streets of the town were located close to the entrance of the castle and the lough shore and a visitor arriving from the direction of Belfast would have entered Carrickfergus by crossing the town defences and going through the gate which would later be known as the West (or Irish) Gate. This gate, located at the western end of modern West Street, was almost certainly of wood, and was a gap in the fortifications that surrounded the town in the Medieval Period. The path on which the visitor walked would have been a dirt track, and shoes and the hems of garments would not have escaped getting dirty.

Once inside, the visitor's attention would have been grabbed immediately by the sights, sounds and smells that were part and parcel of a bustling Medieval town. Unlike modern towns, there was no systematic disposal of rubbish, which was either thrown directly outside the houses or deposited in pits specially dug for the purpose. Some of these pits would have been open, waiting to be filled up, so the smell of rotten food as well as human and animal waste would have been quite overpowering. Other odours that the visitor would have encountered

would have included smoke from fires used to heat the houses within the town, smells of cooking and also those of industrial activity such as pottery making, metal working and brewing. Mixed in with these was the constant salty breeze blowing in off the sea, and the ever-present smell of fish. There must always have been a small fishing fleet – the boats owned by individuals in the town – and fish and crabs would have been part of the staple diet of the inhabitants of Carrickfergus.

St Nicholas' Church from the 1560 map

Walking through the town from the Irish Gate, the visitor would have soon passed the most substantial building within the Medieval town, located to their left between modern Lancasterian Street and Market Place. This was the church of St Nicholas, built in a cruciform shape and sitting within a precinct. This meant that although it was within the town defences, it was set apart from the town itself. Within the ecclesiastical precinct was a Medieval cross and one of the two cemeteries for the townspeople. On the right the visitor would have seen a mixture of buildings that the townspeople lived in. The poorer folk, possibly Irish who had been allowed into the town from the surrounding areas and who would have done the most menial work, lived in structures known as 'beehive' houses. These were flimsy oval-shaped buildings, built of wattle and turf. They were easily and quickly constructed.

The houses of the richer folk, the prominent citizens, merchants and officers of the town garrison were made from a combination of stone and wood.

The townsfolk of Carrickfergus, in constant fear of attack from the Gaelic Irish of south Antrim and north Down (the Clandeboye O'Neills) and from the Highland Scots of the Glens and the Route (the MacDonnells), had three lines of defence: the town ditch and bank with palisade fence, the fortified houses within the town and the castle itself.

The houses of the richer townspeople were arranged around what are the oldest streets in Carrickfergus. They are now known as Essex Street, Cheston Street, Castle Street and High Street. A market cross was located at the junction of Castle Street and High Street, where the market and other outdoor public meetings were held within the town.

At the far end of the town, at the eastern end of modern High Street and just outside the town defences, was the other major ecclesiastical building within Medieval Carrickfergus – the Franciscan Friary. Like St Nicholas' Church, this was located within its own precinct and contained the other cemetery where the townspeople were buried. Late-Medieval maps showed it to be a basic cruciform shape with other buildings built around it. It also had a prominent spire, unlike St Nicholas'.

Carrickfergus was the most important coastal town and port in Ulster and, at any given time in the Medieval Period, there were groups of foreign sailors here on business. Amongst the languages that the visitor could have heard in Medieval

Carrickfergus was Irish (and possibly Scots Gaelic), English (and possibly Lowlands Scots), possibly also French and Spanish. Because it was also for long periods in the Middle Ages, the only town held for the Crown in a part of Ireland that was predominantly Gaelic, it was often reliant on supply by sea. So the visitor would have seen a hive of activity in the harbour, nestling in the shadow of the castle, and filled with boats of all sizes.

'Beehive' houses from the 1560 map

A Medieval boat

The market cross from the 1560 map

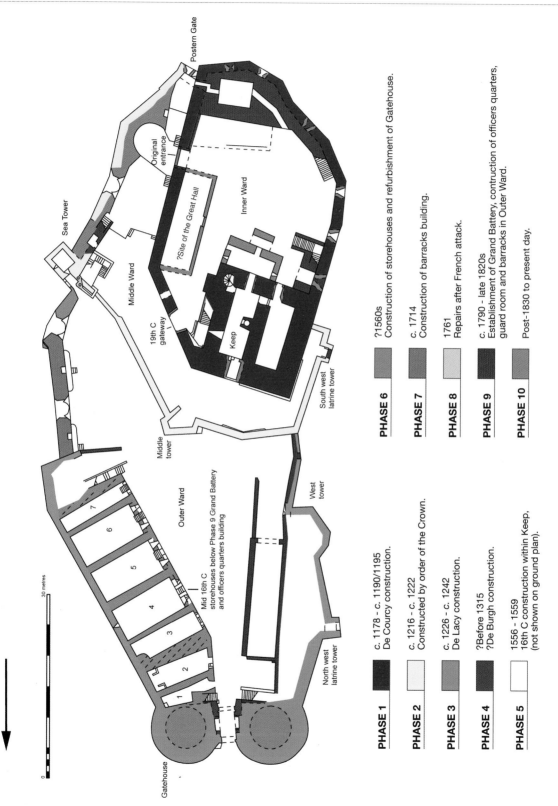

PHASE 1 — c. 1178 - c. 1190/1195
De Courcy construction.

PHASE 2 — c. 1216 - c. 1222
Constructed by order of the Crown.

PHASE 3 — c. 1226 - c. 1242
De Lacy construction.

PHASE 4 — ?Before 1315
?De Burgh construction.

PHASE 5 — 1556 - 1559
16th C construction within Keep,
(not shown on ground plan).

PHASE 6 — ?1560s
Construction of storehouses and refurbishment of Gatehouse.

PHASE 7 — c. 1714
Construction of barracks building.

PHASE 8 — 1761
Repairs after French attack.

PHASE 9 — c. 1790 - late 1820s
Establishment of Grand Battery, contruction of officers quarters,
guard room and barracks in Outer Ward.

PHASE 10 — Post-1830 to present day.

Prepared by E Lennon, R Ó Baoill & N Carver. Based on McNeill 1981.

Plan of Carrickfergus Castle showing the main phases of development

Labels on plan: Postern Gate, Original entrance, Sea Tower, Middle Ward, ?Site of the Great Hall, Inner Ward, 19th C gateway, Keep, South west latrine tower, Middle tower, West tower, North west latrine tower, Outer Ward, Mid 16th C storehouses below Phase 9 Grand Battery and officers quarters building, Gatehouse, 30 metres

5. Focus on Carrickfergus Castle

Introduction

Carrickfergus Castle is probably the best-preserved Medieval castle in Ireland. It is also the castle that had a garrison for the longest period. Construction commenced in the late 12th century and it was only handed over finally to civilian control in 1928. The castle sits on a promontory of sea-girt dolerite stone, which projects out from the north shore of Belfast Lough, next to Carrickfergus town.

The rock on which it sits contains a spring of fresh water which meant that the castle always had a source of clean water. The combination of a good defensive site that could be supplied from both land and sea, the natural harbour for ships that lay beside the promontory and the fresh water available on the rock made the site very attractive to the Anglo-Normans. The port was important for both town and castle, as often they could only be supplied by sea, the overland routes being too dangerous to travel.

Building Materials

The basic stone used in the fabric of the castle buildings was local basalt. To decorate the Medieval buildings, local red sandstone and Cultra limestone were used, especially in the keep and inner ward. Red brick was used for new work and alterations from the 16th century onwards. Large dressed-granite blocks were also used along the east wall and for gun platforms in the 19th century.

The construction of the keep

Development of the Castle

The castle that survives today developed in three phases in less than a century after its formation. The first phase was the initial construction of fortifications on the promontory at Carrickfergus by John de Courcy.

John de Courcy's Castle

In the early decades of its existence, the castle occupied only the southern end of the promontory, with a deep ditch or moat dug into the rock on the northern side. This meant that when the drawbridge was pulled up, the castle was surrounded by water on all sides. The first structures to be built were the keep, the inner ward (an open court or area of a castle enclosed by walls), and the great hall.

The Keep

The keep (or great tower) was the strongest and safest place within the castle, and is located in the north-western corner of the inner ward. Still the most prominent part of the castle, it is almost 20 metres high and has walls between three and four metres thick. Recent archaeological excavations have shown that construction commenced between 1177 and 1181. The main role of the keep was not only defensive, but also to allow the lord and his family a comfortable home. Its height also meant that it could be used as a watchtower from which to look out for enemies approaching the castle, either by land or sea.

Reconstruction of the inner ward at the time of John de Courcy

A feast taking place on the second floor of the keep

The keep has four storeys, each of which was originally reached by a spiral staircase. The ground floor was a vaulted storage cellar and also contained the fresh water well, a guardroom for soldiers and a public latrine. To protect the upper storeys against possible fire and attacks, this floor has no windows. The keep is entered by a stone staircase rising up from the inner ward courtyard to a first floor entrance in the eastern wall. Excavations in 1993 uncovered the remains of the original Cultra sandstone steps and treads and it is clear that the stairs are contemporary with the construction of the east wall of the keep. Visitors to the keep probably waited here for entrance to the private rooms above, and the windows lighting this level were deliberately made small to stop enemies climbing in.

The second floor was originally one large room, where the lord could have entertained or carried out administrative business such as rent collection or court sessions. This floor has a large fireplace and a private latrine, but cross walls were inserted at a later period, blocking some earlier openings. The third floor was where the lord's private chambers

were located, and he and his family lived and slept here. This floor contains large windows, a substantial fireplace and a private latrine. It was heightened and a spanning arch added in the 16th century.

The Inner Ward

The inner ward was, along with the keep, the first part of the castle to be built by John de Courcy. It consists of a high curtain wall enclosing the keep and a small bailey, and excavations have dated this episode in the castle's history to between 1177 and 1181, when the new Anglo-Norman settlement at Carrickfergus was under constant threat from the Irish who lived in the surrounding areas. The surface of the courtyard consists of large basalt boulders deliberately laid down to give a firm base.

The Great Hall

Within the courtyard and opposite the entrance to the keep are the remains of the great hall, where John de Courcy and his wife Affreca would entertain visiting guests. It was a two-storey building with windows overlooking the sea, located beside the entrance gate to the inner ward.

A view of the inner ward from the roof of the keep

A decorated window of the great hall

The area between the keep and the defensive walls of the inner ward would have featured several other buildings constructed of wood and stone, including the kitchens, a small chapel, and a barn and stables for the horses of the lord and his knights. So the ward would have been a place bustling with activity at all times.

The Castle Expands in Size

The castle was enlarged between *circa* 1216 and *circa* 1222, when the fortification was a Crown possession and there was no resident lord. King John clearly wanted to improve the defences to guard against any further attempts by any of his barons to capture the castle and use it as a base for independent action in Ulster.

The walls of the inner and middle wards and the sea tower viewed from the roof of the keep

The Middle Ward

Although now ruined to foundation level, the wall of the middle ward clearly enhanced the defences as well as creating some more room for activity at the castle. There are enough masonry remains left to show that a tower was incorporated into the middle of the northern side of the new wall to provide

Reconstruction of Carrickfergus Castle at the time of John de Courcy

The foundations of the middle ward walls

extra protection for the gate into the castle. A latrine tower is located in the wall, close to the junction with the west wall of the keep. The present gate through the middle ward wall dates to the 19th century.

The Postern Gate

The postern gate was used as an escape route from the castle, but could also be used for soldiers from the garrison to rush out and surprise enemies who were laying siege to the castle. This type of gate is also known as a 'sally port'. Beside the gate is the base of a latrine tower with a double latrine.

The Sea Tower

The sea tower (otherwise known as the north-east angle tower), which is approached down steps, was part of the new defences constructed when the middle ward was created. It was one of four towers originally built along the wall to give archers and the castle garrison control of the outer walls. Later building now blocks two of these towers. The sea tower helped protect the castle from attack from the sea and the surviving arrow slits, of very high quality construction, seem to have been designed for crossbow fire. On the next level was located the castle prison, and

Guarding the postern gate

The sea tower

Reconstruction of the expansion of Carrickfergus Castle between the time of John de Courcy and Hugh de Lacy

The gatehouse

it was from here that the lord of Clandeboye, Con Ó Néill made a dramatic escape in 1604.

Hugh de Lacy's Castle

The Outer Ward

The outer ward was added in the second quarter of the 13th century, after Hugh de Lacy returned to Ireland. The added masonry defences included curtain walls with projecting towers and substantial gate towers on either side of the gate. The new fortifications meant that now the whole of the promontory was occupied by the castle, and that potential attackers would have to fight their way through three heavily-defended gates before they even reached the keep. The added space allowed a bigger garrison to be housed within the castle. Like the inner ward the outer ward probably contained lots of wooden buildings, none of which survives.

The Gatehouse

The gatehouse originally consisted of two circular towers with linking masonry above the gate. Both of the towers had three storeys which were connected by a spiral staircase between the floors.

Cutaway view showing life in the gatehouse

Reconstruction of Carrickfergus Castle as developed by Hugh de Lacy

The gatehouse had to be particularly strong, as it was the only part of the castle not protected by the sea. Although the original was built as part of the outer ward extension to the castle, it was later improved by Richard de Burgh in the early 14th century. Among the improved defences for the gate were arrow slits, a drawbridge pit, a portcullis for trapping enemies within the gate passage and a 'murder hole' for dropping objects on the enemy, once they had been trapped.

In the eastern tower (on the left as you enter the castle), the ground floor was used to store weapons, while the first floor was accommodation for the gatehouse guards. A chapel for the

Windows in the chapel

The castle under siege in 1315

resident lord was located on the upper floor, facing east. In the western tower (to the right of the gate), the ground floor was used to keep prisoners, and the second and third floors were for use by the constable, the military manager of the castle. The second floor was his office and the upper floor his personal quarters.

The Castle Under Siege

During this early period, the most dramatic episode was the year-long siege of the castle by Edward Bruce, when, between 1315 and 1316, his Scottish army invaded Ireland. The impressive defences of the castle kept the Scottish army out and the garrison only surrendered after being driven to starvation when their food had run out and they were unable to get supplies by sea.

The Later History of the Castle

After the murder of the last Earl of Ulster in 1333 and the consequent resurgence of the Irish lords in Ulster, Carrickfergus Castle remained an important administrative centre for much of the Late-Medieval Period. Sometimes it was the only fortification of note held for the Crown in Ulster.

In the 16th century, alterations were made to the castle to make it suitable to mount artillery. Gun ports for cannon, squared off with red brick, were inserted into the east and west walls. The heights of the towers of the gatehouse were lowered and the shape of the towers themselves were altered radically to allow ordnance to be mounted. Despite this, Somhairle Buidhe (Sorley Boy) O'Donnell was able to capture the town and castle in 1575, in revenge for the massacre by the Earl of Essex of 600 mostly women and children on Rathlin Island. In keeping with the type of warfare carried out by the Gaelic Irish and Scots in this period, he would not have held on to the castle for very long, simply plundering it and the town before returning to Gaelic territory.

Sir Arthur Chichester

The town was attacked by the Irish and Scots several times during the later 16th century, and between 1608 and 1615 Sir Arthur Chichester – Governor of Carrickfergus and later Lord Lieutenant of Ireland – had a defensive stone wall constructed around it (see chapter nine). These defences were connected to the outwork defences of the castle.

In the 17th century, Carrickfergus was one of the magazines from which Crown forces acting in the north of Ireland (1600–1652) drew arms, munitions and ordnance. It was also the muster point and magazine for Strafford's 'new army' in 1640. In 1690 the Jacobite garrison in Carrickfergus Castle surrendered to the

Williamite general Frederick Schomberg after his army stormed the town.

On the western rampart of the outer ward are located two cannon dating from the early 18th century and positioned in the brick-built gun ports. These were discovered during excavations in front of the gatehouse in 1951, and are now housed on modern gun carriages.

In January 1754, a 15-metre long section of curtain wall collapsed. This was not properly repaired and, when a

The grand battery

The initials of King George III on a cannon

French expeditionary force attacked Carrickfergus town and castle in 1760, the garrison led a desperate and gallant defence before being allowed to surrender with full honours. This episode will be described in detail in chapter 12.

In the 18th century, parts of the castle were used as a prison. During the 1798 Rebellion it was used as a prison for United Irishmen, including Luke Teeling and William Orr. The castle continued to be used as an armoury and magazine and its armaments were improved during the Napoleonic era in the early 19th century. Six guns on the eastern ('grand') battery date to the scare of invasion during Napoleonic times. They were made in the Carron foundry in Falkirk, Stirlingshire in about 1800 and each bears its individual date, a weight stamp, and the monogram of George III. They are the remnant of a battery of 22 cannon listed as being in the castle in 1811 and placed on the grand battery. Two cannon located below the grand battery at the south-east of the outer ward are also part of the mid-Victorian remodelling of the south-east defences to accommodate 68-pounder muzzle-loader cannon.

Two cannon located between the postern gate and the sea tower also date to the mid-Victorian remodelling of the south-east defences to accommodate four 68-pounder muzzle-loader cannon in elaborate granite emplacements with carriages on swivel rails.

In the early 20th century, during World War I, anti-submarine guns were mounted within the castle on one of the platforms, for defence of Belfast Lough. Finally in 1928, after 750 years of continuous military occupation, the longest of any castle in Ireland, the War Department transferred the castle to the Ministry of Finance for preservation as an ancient monument. Its final military activity came during World War II, when the basements of the keep were used as air-raid shelters.

A 19th-century cannon on the grand battery

A military exercise on the promenade in Victorian times

Carrickfergus Castle: Further Reading

Bigger, F.J. and Fennell, W.J. (1908) 'The round church of Carrig-Fergus Castle', *Ulster Journal of Archaeology*, second series, 14, 183–189

Donnelly, C.J., Ó Néill, J., McNeill, T.E. and McCooey, P. (2005) 'De Courcy's castle: New insights into the first phase of Anglo-Norman building activity at Carrickfergus castle, County Antrim', *Medieval Archaeology*, 49, 311–317

McConnell, C. (2002) *Tales from the Castle Gate: Carrickfergus Castle*, Carrickfergus (Carmac Books)

McNeill, T.E. (1981) *Carrickfergus Castle*, Belfast (HMSO)

Waterman, D.M. (1952) 'Excavations at the entrance to Carrickfergus castle, 1950', *Ulster Journal of Archaeology*, third series, 15, 103–118

6. Late-Medieval Carrickfergus

Introduction

Lead cloth seals

Throughout the Late-Medieval Period, Carrickfergus Castle remained the one stronghold in Ulster held by the English, though one which was attacked by the Irish and Scots on a regular basis. Much of the information on these episodes survives in the State Papers and takes the form of requests from the town for money to rebuild and also for more troops to help defend the outpost. Why the town was not surrounded with a stone defensive wall, as many other Irish towns had been during the Medieval Period, is unclear. Perhaps the precarious nature of the settlement made the Crown unwilling to undertake such a considerable investment. It may also have been thought that the walls of the castle, always the last line of defence for the townspeople, were of sufficient strength and that a stone wall around the town was unnecessary. Finally, the uncertain relations with the Kingdom of Scotland during this period may have put off an investment in substantial town defences that could have been put to use by an invading army, as Edward Bruce had done with Carrickfergus from 1315–18.

Trade

During this period, however, the town continued to trade and was intermittently prosperous. Agricultural products along with hides, wool and sheepskins were the major items that generated income for the earl and the earldom as exports. Records from the time give some indication of the type and level of trade that was being carried on:

- In 1340 a man called Robert de Wryngton and two companions were described as having bought and customed 610 hides at Galway, Carrickfergus and Waterford.
- In 1375 the mayor of Carrickfergus was licensed to import eight weys of wheat and John Wyk, a merchant of the town, imported malt and oats.
- In 1376 James Boys was awarded a two-year licence to bring 60 weys of wheat, oats and other corn from Dublin to Drogheda which was the source of such supplies for Carrickfergus and the other major ports and castles at Carlingford and Greencastle. This highlights the importance of maintaining security along the coast of the Anglo-Norman controlled areas of Ireland, as it was generally the safest route by which supplies and troops could be moved around the country.

A Late-Elizabethan coin

Merchants could make significant profits by selling at inflated prices to the beleaguered inhabitants of places like Carrickfergus. It is clear that from time to time the English government needed to intervene to ensure that supplies reached Carrickfergus. The townspeople sought tax relief in the aftermaths of attacks by the Irish and Scots, and the Crown normally granted these.

Although for much of the period Scotland was regarded as the enemy, trade – both legal and illicit – also took place with the Scots. In 1403–04 a Carrickfergus merchant was granted licences to export corn, flour, salt-meat and beer to the Scots. There are also references to illicit trade in wine that had been imported for use by the castle garrison. Presumably this type of trade was carried on with the local Irish as well, illustrating the isolated position of Carrickfergus throughout the Medieval Period and the desperate methods that were needed to generate money for the earldom and the merchants of the town. It is possible that commodities being produced in the iron and pottery industries of Carrickfergus, evidence of which has been uncovered during excavations within the town, were also being traded and exported during this period.

Carrickfergus in Turbulent Times

In 1384 Carrickfergus town was burnt by Niall O'Neill, a sign of the declining power of the Anglo-Norman earldom and the emerging power of the Gaelic lords in the surrounding areas. Two years later, in 1386, the town was burnt by the Highland Scots, and a request from the mayor and burgesses of Carrickfergus to the lord deputy Robert de Vere, Marquis of Dublin, to 'build and repair it' in the following year may refer to either or both attacks. In 1402

Medieval transport

the Highland Scots again attacked the town, and it was reported that Carrickfergus had been 'totally burnt by our enemies'. The colony was reported as only surviving by paying 'black rent' to the Clandeboye O'Neills in 1460, and the townsfolk had probably worked out a *modus vivendi* with the local Irish and Highland Scots. Commodities such as wine and cloth that were being imported into the town would also have been desired by the Irish and Scots, who could then acquire them through trade with the merchants of the town. Consequently, it did not suit the Irish or the Highland Scots to completely destroy Carrickfergus, even if they had been able.

During the 16th century the town seemed to be in almost constant danger of being overrun. In 1507, another Niall O'Neill, Chief of the Clandeboye O'Neills, was captured by the townspeople of Carrickfergus and was only released in exchange for O'Neill hostages. However, on his release he immediately returned in force, attacked the town, captured the castle and the mayor of Carrickfergus and released the hostages. A few years later, in 1513, a Scottish naval expedition against England attacked and plundered Carrickfergus while passing the coast, the actual description stating that they set 'Craigfergus into fyre, and safet neither barne nor byre'. The perilous situation is reflected in the fact that the

Gaelic warrior

Irish Galloglas drawn by Dürer in the 16th century

castle is listed as having only four horsemen in 1549–50. In 1556, Carrickfergus was attacked again by the Highland Scots under the leadership of James MacDonnell.

Against the backdrop of such turbulence, renewed building activity in the castle was carried out in the 16th century, with alterations made for defence against and for use of artillery. Red brick was used in the alterations, though much of the brick work still visible today is from a later date.

Early Maps of the Town

Two maps of Carrickfergus survive from this time. The first, drawn *circa* 1560, is the earliest map of any town in Ulster. The perspective is quite strange, with the town viewed from the south-western, seaward side. Like many maps of this period, it was probably sketched out on board a ship and details of the town added later. It depicts the defensive ditch around the town, and St Nicholas' Church located inside the line of the town defences within its own enclosure with the stump of a high cross visible, presumably indicating a cemetery. The Franciscan Friary is shown at the far end of the town, just outside the town boundary, with its associated buildings and cemetery, and again within its own enclosure. A stream flowing from above the town runs along the eastern defences and down to the sea, perhaps evidence of the mill mentioned in a lease of 1403–04. Another stream is illustrated originating in one of the associated buildings of the friary, probably denoting the presence of another mill or a drainage channel. This again was referred to in written references in the 15th century.

The map shows twelve fortified stone buildings or tower houses (one of which is circular) within the town, as well as conjoined longer, single-storey buildings. These are shown as running back from the castle as far as the friary, on either side of a street, presumably modern High Street. In the middle of the street, at the castle end, stands a stone market cross. Between the tower houses and St Nicholas' Church, and also strung out along the shore, are shown the beehive houses of the poorer residents living within the town.

Within the castle, cannon are shown mounted in the inner and outer wards (ramparts of the south wall of the outer ward). The backs of both gatehouse towers seem to be in disrepair or else in the process of being modified. However, no gun ports are portrayed in the castle walls. There are buildings in the outer ward portrayed as both roofed (against the north wall) and unroofed (on the rampart of the south wall), and the whole of the interior of the castle is shown as having a cobbled surface. In the harbour are six boats of various sizes and the pier seems to consist of large numbers of upright timbers with the interior filled with stones.

The map seems very stylised with no attempt to portray any effects of warfare on the town, so that both the church and friary are shown as roofed. This is not the case with the map of the town drawn only a few years later in 1567 by Robert Lythe, which is altogether more detailed. It is viewed from the south, with the town alignment more easily recognisable.

Lythe's map shows the frame of a gallows outside the line of the town's defensive ditch, to the north-west of the town. Within the limits of the town there are descriptions of some of the earlier defences and buildings from the Anglo-Norman Period, now obsolete ('an old trench where a mill hath stande' ...'an old trenche' ... 'another olde trenche').

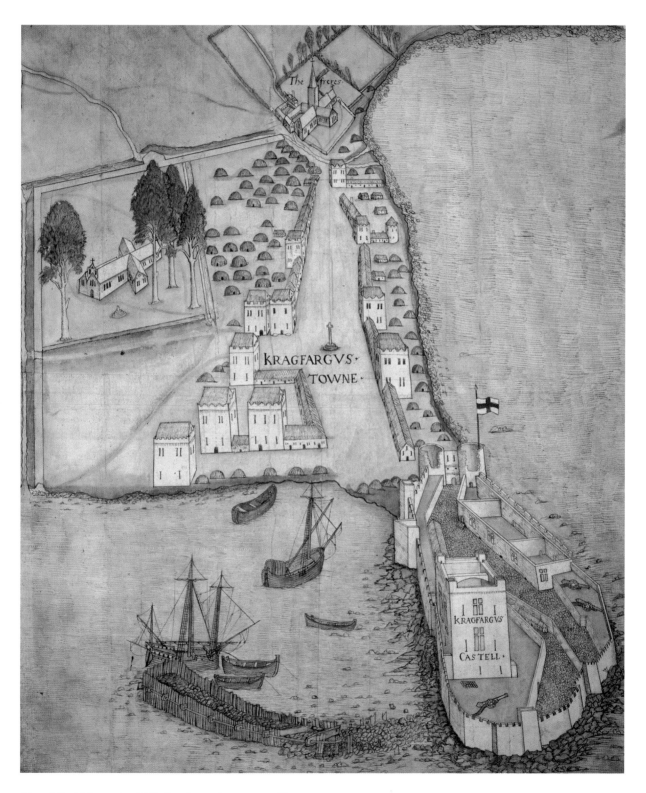

Map of Carrickfergus circa 1560 (BL Cotton Augustus I ii 42)

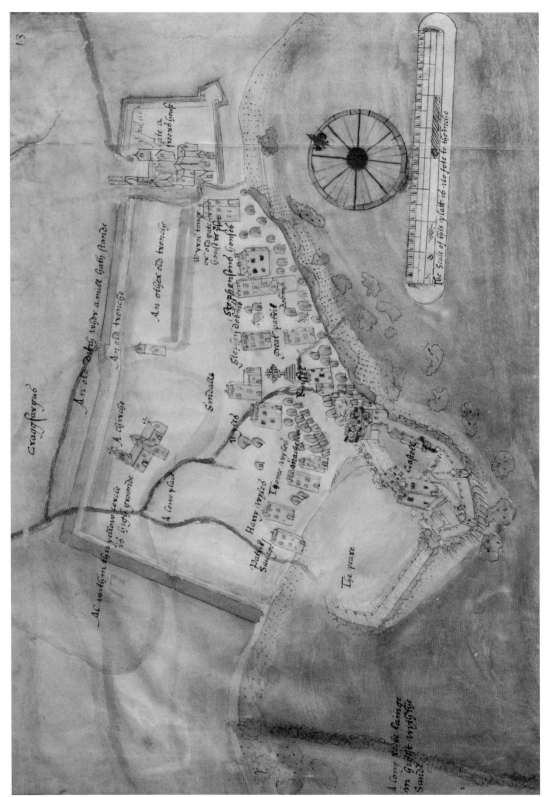

Map of Carrickfergus in 1567 by Robert Lythe (Trinity College, Dublin, MS 1209 (26))

There are also attempts to give topographical information ('all within this yellow circle is high ground' …'a lowe place').

St Nicholas' Church ('a churche') is portrayed as roofless, with crosses on all four gables. A stream is shown flowing to the sea to the west of the castle, and also through the centre of the town. To the east of St Nicholas' Church, a long and roofless building with pointed gables, aligned north-south might be one of the lost ecclesiastical buildings founded in the Anglo-Norman Period, perhaps the Premonstratensian Abbey. This is the only map known to portray this building.

On the east of the town, the buildings of the Franciscan Friary are now described as 'The Pallace. Late a Friar's House'. The suppression of religious houses in Ireland commenced in 1537 with the Reformation. However, the friary in Carrickfergus seems to have survived until Elizabeth I ascended the throne in 1558 and was probably seized soon after. In the years following, it was converted into a fortified storehouse and strong point in the north-eastern sector of the town, 'The Pallace'.

A bastion is shown at the south-eastern corner of the defences enclosing the building.

The 1567 map also portrays a stream originating at one of the buildings in the 'Pallace' complex, implying that the mill from the friary was still in use. The friary/'Pallace' is now incorporated inside the line of the town defences, showing that the limits of the town had expanded to the east.

Closer to the centre of Carrickfergus a number of streets – Cheston Street,

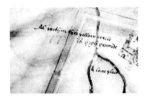

The town gallows portrayed on 1567 map

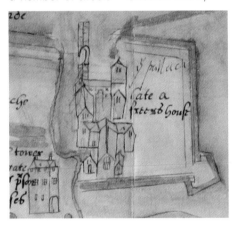

The 'Pallace' (formerly the Franciscan friary) on the 1567 map

St Nicholas' Church on the 1567 map

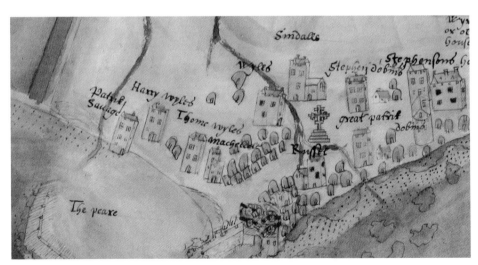

Detail of 1567 map showing the town streets and various types of houses

The market cross from the 1567 map

Castle Street and High Street – are now discernible, but not clearly mapped out by the layout of the tower houses around them. Twelve or thirteen tower houses are illustrated, and the names of most of the occupants – the most prominent men of the town – are listed. The names include those of Patrick Savage, Harry Wyles, Thomas Wyles, Stephen Dobins along with those of the Sindall, Dobins and Stephenson families. The circular tower is still shown as surviving and once more some tower houses are portrayed as having attached buildings.

Archaeological excavations over the last 35 years have uncovered the structural remains of two of the tower houses from this period. The first one, excavated in 1972 at Cheston Street, was identified as the house of Henry Wyles, marked on the 1567 map of Carrickfergus. Amongst the high-status artefacts recovered was a 16th-century copper-alloy brooch.

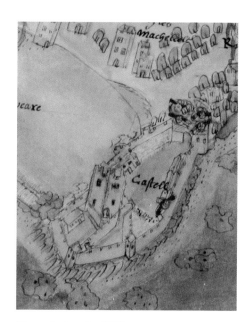

The castle from the 1567 map

The second tower house was investigated in 1973–74 and was located underneath no. 37 High Street. The building was almost square in plan, approximately 6.5 metres by 7 metres, and with walls 1.25 metres thick. A possible internal wall was also uncovered during the excavation. A 15th- or 16th-century masonry windowhead was found in demolition rubble at the site and is probably related to the tower house. High-status finds included fragments of wine glasses, coins, a spearhead, a lead weight box and an 'official' copper-alloy weight.

Dendrochronological examination of timbers found in the building dated it to the period 1560–67. Since it is depicted on the 1567 map, it would appear to have been the dwelling of Thomas Stephenson, who was mayor of Carrickfergus on several occasions.

The market cross called 'Great Patrick' is still visible on the map, and a building, the 'Wyrol Tower' or old gatehouse or prison, is located at the

Shane O'Neill

The common seal of Carrickfergus

Kilclief Tower House

eastern end of modern High Street. The beehive houses are again shown throughout the centre of the town and along the shoreline.

The castle is portrayed with a small building in the inner ward and larger ones in the outer ward and the map shows cannon sited on the rampart of the outer ward and on both gatehouses.

Carrickfergus in the Elizabethan Period

Writing about Ulster in the 1560s, when Shane O'Neill of Tyrone was the most powerful Irish lord there, Lord Deputy Sir Henry Sidney noted that Shane O'Neill:

… held in his subjection the lordship and lords of Clandeboy and the Route; the Scotts of the Glynnes he held in his pay and they were his mercenary soldiers. The Queen [Elizabeth 1] had nothing in possession in all this large tract of land but the miserable town of Carregfergus, whose goodes he would take as ofte as he listed, and force the poor people to redeeme their owne cowes with their owne wyne.

Carrickfergus retained its urban status throughout the Medieval Period. The town was given a charter by Elizabeth 1 in 1568, but probably had an earlier one, now lost. During the 16th- and 17th-century plantations, Antrim and Down were not escheated (confiscated by the Crown). Because of its location, Carrickfergus became a centre of government administration and for the mustering of armies. With renewed English interest in the Irish lands in Ulster in the 1570s, there were two botched attempts to seize or settle parts of Antrim and Down. In 1571 Elizabeth 1 granted much of eastern Ulster to

Thomas Smith, the earliest attempt at plantation in Ulster. Smith's plans ended in disaster, but the Clandeboye O'Neills, whose lands were targeted, were so aggrieved that they attacked and burned Carrickfergus in 1573. Walter Deveraux, the first Earl of Essex then planned to colonise those parts of southern and eastern Antrim not within the borough of Carrickfergus. However, his plans also came to nothing.

In 1575 Carrickfergus was again attacked by the Highland Scots, Somhairle Buidhe (Sorley Boy) MacDonnell. The castle was taken and the town burnt (including St Nicholas' church) in revenge for Essex's massacre of MacDonnell women and children on Rathlin Island.

With the arrival in 1575 of the new Lord Deputy, Sir Henry Sidney, there were concerted efforts to reinvigorate the defences of Carrickfergus. Sidney describes the town as it was when he first arrived:

The Towne of Carrickfergus, I found moche decaied and impoverished, no Ploughs going at all, where before were manye, and great Store of Kyne and Cattle, beloynge to the Towne, nowe few or none lefte, Churche and howsies, saving

The late-16th-century town wall uncovered at Essex Street

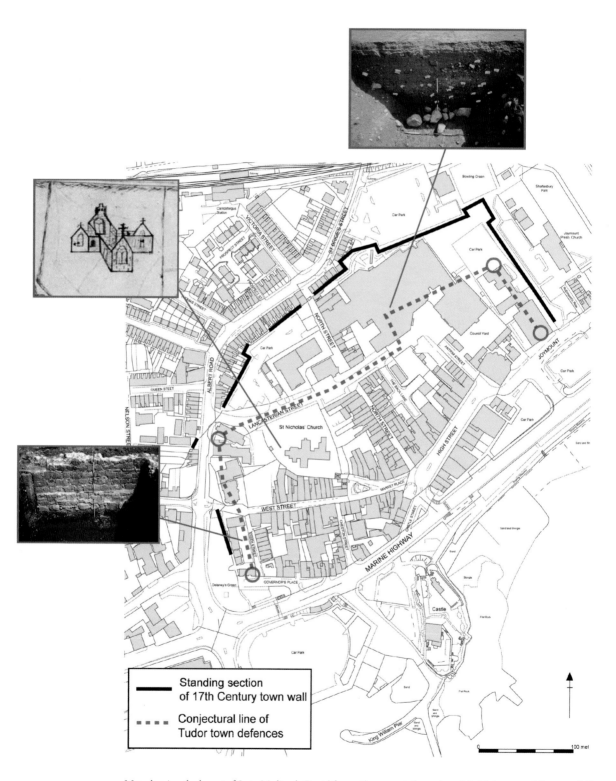

Map showing the layout of Late-Medieval Carrickfergus, the excavated remains of the Tudor town defences and St Nicholas' Church (from the 1596 map)

Castells [tower houses] burned; the Inhabiteants fled, not above five Howseholders of any Countenance leaft remayninge; …

The first attempts to improve the situation at Carrickfergus involved reviving the old Medieval earthen bank and ditch defences which were altered in 1574 by the building of a '… vamour of sods and turf [a bank] … with 4 mounts [circular bastions] at the corners [of the town]'.

A rectangular bastion was also constructed at the south-eastern corner of the 'Pallace'.

The defensive circuit was completed between 1574–79 by the building of a stone sea wall to both the east and west of the castle, along the shore and as far as the Irish/West Gate entrance into the town.

Archaeological excavations within the town have uncovered sections of the later 16th-century Tudor defences. At Essex Street, in the west of the town, a seven-metre long stretch of the stone wall and extra-mural ditch were uncovered in 1991–92. The wall, which was founded on a substantial offset plinth, stood to a height of 2.5 metres and was located just below the modern street surface. It was at least 1.5 metres thick and was constructed in courses of roughly-cut and heavily-mortared basalt stones with small split stones inserted in between them to keep the coursing level. The extra-mural ditch was roughly 4 metres wide and 1.3 metres deep.

Evidence for the town bank and ditch, which enclosed some six to seven hectares, was uncovered during excavations by Tom Delaney at Joymount in 1973–74, and by the author at Lancasterian Street in 1995. These took the form of an earthen bank with boulder foundations and a ditch

approximately 5.5 metres wide. At Lancasterian Street, the upper levels of the town ditch had been filled in with construction debris from the building of the later 17th-century stone wall, as the town expanded northwards. The 16th-century defences at the eastern side of the town diverged from the Medieval line, running roughly parallel to, but 10 metres back from, the later eastern stone wall of the town. None of the mounts or circular bastions has yet been located, so the form of their construction remains uncertain.

The Town at the End of the 16th Century

The increasing English involvement in the affairs of Gaelic Ireland led to a prolonged period of warfare, the Nine Years War (1593–1603), with most of Ulster in open revolt. A map of Carrickfergus drawn *circa* 1596 illustrates the changes that the town had undergone during the second half of the 16th century. The town is now shown as being partially walled along the seaward side and as far as the Irish Gate on the western side. A small stretch of walling is also evident at the northern side of the 'Pallace'. Only one of the four circular mounts (the south-

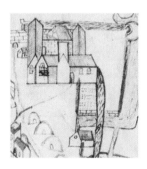

'The Palace' from the 1596 map

A Gaelic lord feasting

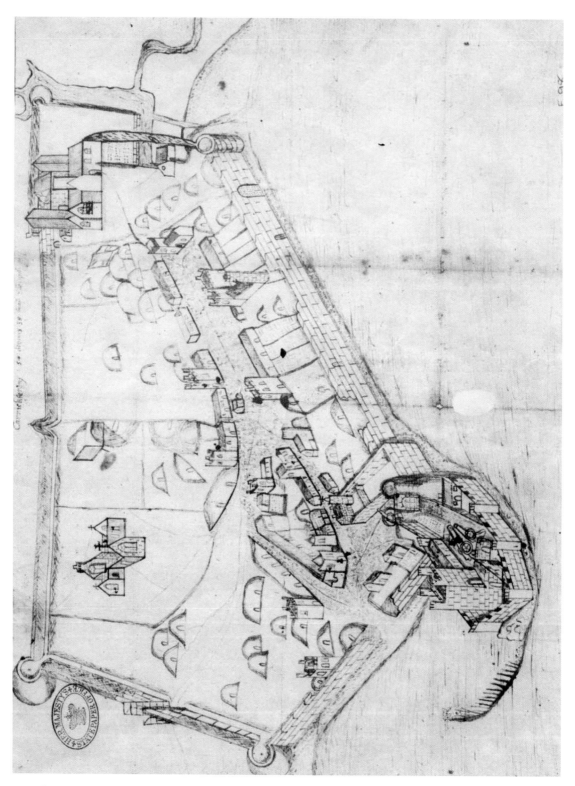

Map of Carrickfergus circa 1596 (Public Record Office, London, MPF 98 (ex 64/1/31))

eastern) is portrayed as being built in stone. The others were presumably of earthen construction, even though another (the south-western) is shown at the junction of two stretches of stone wall. The main town defences along the north-western, northern and eastern sides of the town still appear to be earthen bank-and-ditch construction.

St Nicholas' Church is once more depicted as roofless. A square outline to the east of it may again be an attempt to mark the site of the building, possibly a church, marked on the 1567 map, but this is uncertain. The complex of buildings that were formerly the Franciscan Friary but now the fortified 'Pallace' is again portrayed. Water is again shown as flowing through the complex, so presumably the mill was still in operation at this time.

There is more detail of the divisions within the town than on previous maps. The roads known today as West Street, Cheston Street, Castle Street and High Street are now visible. The Irish Gate and two other openings in the sea wall, on either side of the castle, are clearly illustrated. Property boundaries within the town are also now marked for the first time.

In the centre of the town twelve tower houses linked by smaller terraced houses are shown, but none of the owners' names are given as was done on the 1567 map. The market cross (Great Patrick) seems to have been removed by this time. The beehive houses of the poorer people are still evident throughout the town and some of these are portrayed as quite large structures. A stone building with a stone wall enclosure to the rear is shown in front of the entrance to the castle.

The map shows cannon mounted in the outer ward of the castle and on top

of one of the gatehouses. Two pitched-roof buildings, on either side of the outer ward, are also shown within the castle, while immediately to the west, the pier of the harbour is depicted by an upright row of timbers.

The Battle of Altfracken

In 1597, the year after the map was drawn, Sir John Chichester was appointed Governor of Carrickfergus. He appears to have come to Ireland in the early 1590s, and before serving at Carrickfergus was employed as a Sergeant Major in the English army in Ireland. His appointment to Carrickfergus, the only major fortified settlement held by the Crown in Ulster at this time, came when the forces of Gaelic Ireland were having their most successful period during the Nine Years War.

Chichester managed to re-take two castles (Belfast and Edenduffcarrick/ Shane's Castle) before disaster struck, brought about by Sir James MacDonnell and the Highland Scots of the Route and Glens. The MacDonnells, with their power base at Dunluce Castle near Ballycastle, played an ambiguous role during the Nine Years War. Though Gaelic in culture and language, they still had strong links with Scotland and the court of King James. The Crown was never sure of their allegiance and, as a consequence, harassed and raided their lands on a regular basis. The MacDonnells, in response, raided down as far as Carrickfergus.

In an effort to resolve this situation (and give him one less enemy to deal with), Sir John Chichester arranged a parley with Sir James MacDonnell for November 4th 1597 near Carrickfergus at Altfracken (Ballycarry), to which both sides brought numbers of armed men as a precaution. However, incited by his

Detail of streets in the town from the 1596 map

'Beehive' houses from the 1596 map

The castle shown from the 1596 map

Sir John Chichester

A Gaelic soldier

Hugh O'Neill, Earl of Tyrone

junior officers, Chichester led the English cavalry in a charge against the Scots forces. This unprovoked attack was a badly-managed affair and in the battle that followed, MacDonnell's men soundly defeated the troops from Carrickfergus. Sir John Chichester was killed, his body decapitated and his head sent to Hugh O'Neill, Earl of Tyrone and the principal leader of the Gaelic armies in Ireland, who was based at Dungannon.

After this debacle the Highland Scots or Irish could probably have captured Carrickfergus, and why they did not is still a mystery, although it may in part have been lack of confidence on the part of the Gaelic armies in their ability to capture well-fortified towns. More likely, it was part of the O'Neill policy at that period of the Nine Years War to try and force the English out of Gaelic Ulster without provoking an all-out war. The destruction of Carrickfergus would have demanded an extreme response by the Crown, and so they pulled back from it.

In April 1599, Sir Arthur Chichester, the brother of the slain Sir John Chichester, was appointed Governor of Carrickfergus. His arrival ushered in a new era in the history of the town. Apart from John de Courcy, Sir Arthur Chichester was probably the single most important individual connected with the development of Carrickfergus. His story and the resurrected fortunes of Carrickfergus town in the 17th century will be told in chapter 9.

7. A Walk Through Late-Medieval Carrickfergus

A visitor to Late-Medieval Carrickfergus at the end of the 16th century would have found the town a fortified port and settlement, in keeping with the turbulent times that Ireland found itself in. There would have been larger numbers of soldiers and cavalry visible than in previous times, and there would have been a more pronounced feeling of danger and of the town being on a war footing.

Carrickfergus having suffered its most sustained number of attacks in the second half of the 16th century did not escape undamaged. Walking through the town the visitor would have come across many examples of buildings damaged by the repeated attacks on the town. Among these would have been St Nicholas' Church, now roofless and neglected, and the friary (the 'Pallace'), suppressed after the Reformation, and now converted into a fortified storehouse.

However, alongside damage and decay the visitor would have found evidence of prosperity and growth. The most notable examples would have been the presence of some twelve tower houses, located along the main thoroughfares in the centre of the town. These were defended stone houses –'mini castles' – that had been built mostly in the 15th century by the principal merchants and dignitaries of the town. In fact, the town and castle were viewed by the Crown as a single fortified unit in this period, and it was decided that a larger garrison was needed for their protection.

The visitor would also have noted that high-status goods and products still abounded in the town, and it would have been clear to them that although the town was under severe threat for much of this period, high-quality pottery and other personal effects were still being imported into the town. It is evident that the quality of life, at least for the richer citizens, was good, despite periods of hardship.

The Saint Nicholas stained glass window

8. Focus on St Nicholas' Church

Introduction

St Nicholas' Church dominates the centre of Carrickfergus and the area around Market Place, North Street and Lancasterian Street. It stands on a slight rise some 200 metres to the north-west of the castle. Although over 800 years old, it is still used as a place of worship by the Church of Ireland. St Nicholas' is one of Ulster's most important churches and one of the few Medieval churches with its roof still intact.

The original entrance of the church faces Carrickfergus Castle and can be approached from High Street via Market Place. Access is now possible from Lancasterian Street, a later development.

The church tower and spire seen from Lancasterian Street

A view of St Nicholas' Church and town from the roof of the castle keep

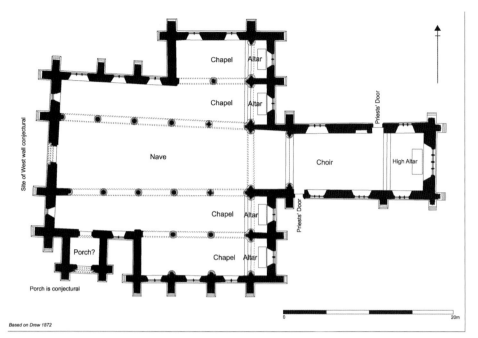

A plan of how St Nicholas' Church may have been laid out in the early 14th century, drawn by Sir Thomas Drew

Old black and white photographs of St Nicholas' Church

The Environment and Heritage Service: Built Heritage regards St Nicholas' Church as a monument of great significance. The church is a Grade A listed monument with Scheduled Monument protected status. It is entered into the Northern Ireland Historic Buildings Record as HB22/08/001.

In the history of St Nicholas' there have been four main periods of construction – two in the Medieval Period, one occurring in the early 17th century under Sir Arthur Chichester, and the last in the late 19th century.

The History of St Nicholas' Church

John De Courcy built St Nicholas' church in the late 12th century as the parish church of the new Anglo-Norman settlement of Carrickfergus. It was built in the Cistercian style, common at the time, and dedicated to St Nicholas. In

1306 the church was enlarged and completed by Robert le Mercer, who was responsible for the unusually long choir. By this time, the church was held in such esteem that a special papal tax was imposed to maintain it.

As discussed earlier, the first town map in Ulster was of Carrickfergus and was produced around 1560. This

Interior view of the nave

Interior view of the chancel

St Nicholas' Church from the circa 1560 map

The roof timbers

Sir Thomas Drew

A Medieval tile from St Nicholas' Church

shows how important the settlement was at that time. Unfortunately, it was also almost 400 years after town and church were established, so the evolution of the building during the Medieval and Late-Medieval Periods has not been recorded.

Only fragments of the Anglo-Norman church have survived the last 800 years. These take the form of a number of piers on either side of the nave and most of the north-east crossing pier. These piers had elaborate mouldings at the crossings. Medieval fragments built into the present walls show that the original church was much larger and wider than the present one. There were arcades between the nave and the aisles and substantial arches opening out on both sides of the nave, leading to the side aisles and chapels.

The eminent architect, Sir Thomas Drew, carried out restoration work at St. Nicholas' in the 1870s. The evidence of the earlier chapels was noted by him in his report on the new works where he describes that:

...opposite the two east ward arches on each side would appear to have been lateral chapels, two on the south and two on the north, which occupied very nearly the area of the present transepts. ...

The position of these chapels would have been about the east walls of the present transepts.

Archaeological excavations carried out by Tom Delaney at nos 11–17 Market Place in 1972 uncovered Medieval burials, suggesting that the Medieval cemetery attached to the church was also considerably larger than that of today. He also uncovered decorated floor tiles and painted window glass from the church itself.

St Nicholas' seems to have fallen into decay in the Late-Medieval Period. On the 1560 map, the church is portrayed as cruciform in shape, with a side aisle to the north and an entrance through the western gable. In the slightly later 1567 map of Carrickfergus, St Nicholas' is shown as having two entrances on the south wall and a small tower on the western gable. In 1568 documentary sources record that some repairs were made to St Nicholas' by Sir Henry Sidney, but it is uncertain what these were. On the 1596 map of the town St Nicholas' is portrayed as roofless, following the attacks of the 1570s.

Substantial restoration did not recommence until the first quarter of the 17th century, when Sir Arthur Chichester had the transepts rebuilt under the direction of master mason Thomas Paps. This is more or less the church as we see it today. The 17th-century works either removed or obscured a lot of the earlier church. Paps encased the Medieval piers and much of the Anglo-Norman masonry in the new walls, in some cases strengthening but more often masking the earlier Medieval work. These were not uncovered again until work carried out on the church in 1907. Paps built the north aisle with its raised floor as a chapel and burial vault for his family.

The chancel is now much longer than when originally built by Robert le Mercer. Below the crossing at the transepts the nave is 12.5 metres long, while beyond the crossing the chancel extends for 22.5 metres. The original roof was also lower, and the floor of the church is approximately one metre higher than the original, due to various roof collapses and the several restorations throughout its history.

The window openings of the choir are largely the same as the original Anglo-Norman building. There were four on the south, the great window on the east and two on the north side. The east window still retains the banded shafts on the interior window jambs from which spring moulded arches. The only side window which has original stone work is at the north-east corner.

The church contains the Chichester Memorial, constructed of marble and alabaster, which depicts Arthur Chichester, his wife, son, and brother, and survives as one of the most sophisticated pieces of Jacobean architecture in Ireland. Sir Arthur Chichester was Governor of Carrickfergus, Lord Deputy of Ireland and a successful soldier in the Nine

Years War (1593–1603). The Chichester family became Earls of Donegall and landlords of much of County Antrim, including Belfast.

The roof of the Chichester Transept is barrel-vaulted, while the rest of the church roof is constructed of timber. This is clearly not original, perhaps dating to the Victorian Period and the work of Sir Thomas Drew.

Later changes include the replacement of Tudor brickwork with Portland stone and the replacement of the old steeple in 1787. The tower, with its octagonal spire and modern clock face, now consists of a classical pedimented doorway topped by a tripartite Palladian window. This Georgian work has great similarities with the steeple of Holy Trinity Church (Church of Ireland) in Ballycastle, dating to *circa 1756*.

As noted earlier, Sir Thomas Drew carried out conservation in the 1870s. In the 20th century, members of the Tower of Glass studio in Dublin inserted

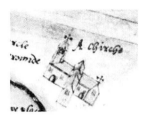

St Nicholas's Church on the 1567 map

St Nicholas's Church on the 1596 map

Sir Arthur Chichester

The classical pedimented doorway

The tripartite Palladian window

Sir Thomas Drew's drawing of the interior of the Medieval church

stained glass windows of outstanding quality. *The Good Samaritan*, the *Good Shepherd* and the *Prodigal Son* are all by Lady Glenavy (1912). *Saint Andrew* (1929) is by Catherine O'Brien, and *Saints Columba, Patrick* and *Aidan* (1912) and *Saint John* (1929) are both by Ethel Rhind.

A Tour of St Nicholas'

The church that exists today, therefore, is a fascinating mixture of architectural styles that represent its 800-year life. The various different features of the church are now described for the visitor entering from the east porch and taking a tour of the building in a clockwise direction. The numbers in brackets refer to their location on the plan of St Nicholas' that accompanies this chapter.

The Medieval stone cross

The East Porch and Vestries

The east porch and vestry room, where modern entry to the church is now gained through the north-east wall of the church [1], were originally built by Dean Dobbs in 1787 over the vault of the Dobbs family, one of the most

The Williamite cannonball

prominent families in the long history of Carrickfergus. A stone cross that sits on the ledge in the porch was uncovered during works carried out in the church and would have originally sat on top of a gable wall. A cannon ball also on display in the porch was discovered in the graveyard and dates to the Williamite siege of the town in 1689.

The Chancel [2]

Of the seven windows in the chancel only one is original and that was restored by the late Edwin Darley Hill.

The carved wooden table

A visitor entering the chancel will find directly on their left the sanctuary with its beautifully carved wooden holy table. The bishop's pastoral staff in the

The Carrickfergus Borough coat of arms above the chancel entrance

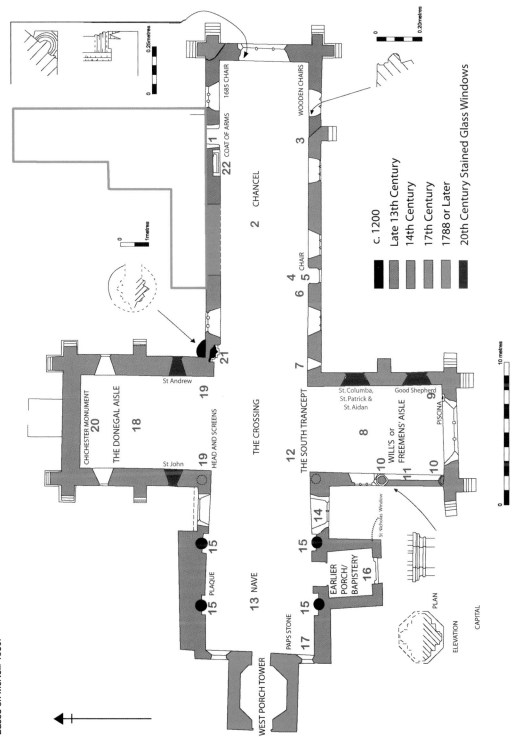

Prepared by E.Lennon, R.Ó Baoill and N.Carver. Based on McNeill 1980.

0.25metres

1metres

0 0.20metres

c. 1200

Late 13th Century

14th Century

17th Century

1788 or Later

20th Century Stained Glass Windows

1685 CHAIR

22 COAT OF ARMS

1 1

2 CHANCEL

WOODEN CHAIRS

3

4 5 CHAIR

6 7

St Andrew

21

19

CHICHESTER MONUMENT

20

THE DONEGAL AISLE

18

St John

19

HEAD AND SCREENS

THE CROSSING

St. Columba, St. Patrick & St. Aidan

Good Shepherd

9

PISCINA

12

THE SOUTH TRANCEPT

8

WILL'S or FREEMENS' AISLE

10

11

10

St. Nicholas Window

14

15

15

PLAQUE

15

13 NAVE

EARLIER PORCH/ BAPISTERY

16

15

17

PAPS STONE

WEST PORCH TOWER

CAPITAL

PLAN

ELEVATION

10 metres

0

Plan of St Nicholas' Church, showing the various phases of building and architectural features described in the text

The staff of Bishop John Frederick MacNeice

The upright Medieval grave slab in the chancel of St Nicholas' Church

MacNeice, Bishop MacNeice was Rector of Carrickfergus from 1908–31.

The Upright Medieval Grave Slab [3]

On the south wall beside the sanctuary, opposite the entrance doorway, is one of the few surviving Anglo-Norman sandstone cross slabs in Carrickfergus. A second lies recumbent in the north wall of the chancel [22]. They originally would have covered a grave. This type of coffin lid is trapezoidal in shape and dates to the 13th century. Such lids were often decorated with foliate crosses and sometimes also with a sword or shears to denote either a male or female burial. They are only found in south-eastern County Antrim and eastern County Down, in the coastal areas controlled by the Anglo-Normans. The sandstone used for the grave slabs was quarried at Scrabo, just outside Newtownards in County Down, and appears to have been distributed by boat from Newtownards throughout the earldom.

The 17th-century Chair and the 'Priest's Door'

Further along the south wall of the chancel is a highly decorated wooden

northern side of the sanctuary was that used by the late John Frederick MacNeice, Bishop of Down, Connor and Dromore. Father of the poet Louis

Anglo-Norman grave slabs at Movilla Abbey, Co. Down

A 17th-century chair in St Nicholas' Church

The Thomas Couper memorial

chair, with the initials 'R B' and the date '1659'. An attached plaque states that the chair originally belonged to Robert Butcher of West Street, Carrickfergus [4].

The chair is located in front of a blocked-up entrance in the south chancel wall [5]. This doorway is known as the 'priest's door' and appears to be Medieval in origin. Tradition says that it is the entrance that the monks used for their daily services.

Above the blocked-up door is a plaque and crest commemorating Thomas Couper [6], alderman and twice mayor of Carrickfergus, who died in 1625.

Further along the south chancel wall is located a very low, narrow window beside the prayer desk. This is the 'leper window' or low side window [7]. Of Anglo-Norman date, it seems to have been inserted after the chancel was constructed.

The Wills' Aisle [8]

This aisle is a reminder of the prominent family who lived in the town. Several tower houses on the 1567 map of Carrickfergus appear to have been owned or lived in by the Wyles family, although none of these dwellings now survives.

This south transept is also known as 'freeman's aisle' because the freemen of Carrickfergus sat here for the services. They were obliged to go to church every Sunday with the mayor. On the right of this aisle, at the front, were the seats of the mayor, aldermen and burgesses. In those days they sat in state behind an arcade, which divided the aisle from the crossing. This arcading was removed during the restoration of 1872.

One of the most interesting links with the past is found low down on the left. It is a Medieval 'piscina' in which the vessels were washed after the sacrament of the Mass [9]. It contains a small drain hole leading into the ground.

The Anglo-Norman 'leper window'

In the western wall of the Wills' Aisle are the remains of two Medieval columns from the 14th century [10]. On the window sill between these lie a number of carved stones [11]. Apart from two that formed a window head in Wills' Castle, they all reportedly come from the now lost Anglo-Norman abbey at Woodburn with which St Nicholas' Church was linked.

The Crossing

The font of the church [12] is located in the crossing, close to the junction of the south wall of the nave and the east wall of the Wills' Aisle. The font is constructed of high-quality Egyptian porphyry. It is badly cracked, damage which has been attributed to French soldiers when they stormed and occupied the town in February 1760.

The Nave [13]

The nave was rebuilt under the direction of Sir Arthur Chichester in 1614. At the eastern end of the south wall is a 16th-century Flemish window depicting Christ being baptised in the River Jordan by John the Baptist [14]. This is not an original feature of the church but was removed from the private chapel of Dangan House, County Meath, and was given as a gift to the parish in about 1800.

Four of the original Anglo-Norman pillars are also visible in both the southern and northern walls of the nave [15].

The Baptistery [16]

The baptistery is located off the southern side of the nave. It was constructed by Thomas Paps in 1614 as the entrance porch of the church and served this function from 1614 to 1778, when the new tower was built. Church porches were places where civil business was transacted and where coroner's courts were held. Public deeds and covenants were signed there and the first part of the marriage service,

Exterior view of the baptistery

One of the Medieval piers surviving within the Nave walls

The font

The 16th-century Flemish window in the south wall of the nave

being a contract, also took place in it. This porch was closed up in 1778 and used as a family tomb. In 1952 the feature was made into a baptistery, and the present cut stone font may originally have come from the now lost Medieval abbey at Woodburn.

The reconstruction of the nave is commemorated by a stone tablet near the back on the southern wall [17]. It states that:

> This worke begune 1614, Mr. Cooper then Maior, and wrought by Thomas Paps freemason, Mr. Openshaw being Parson: Vivat Rex Jacobus.

The Chichester or Donegall Aisle

The Chichester Aisle [18] was constructed in 1614 as the burial vault of the family of Sir Arthur Chichester, and several of the Chichester family are interred there. It is the northern aisle or transept opposite the Will's Aisle. Originally entered from the nave by a

The Thomas Paps stone tablet in the nave

door that is now built up, it is a barrel-roofed vault in cut red sandstone. At the entrance to the aisle are two heavily decorated wooden screens, dating from the 17th century [19].

The Chichester Memorial [20] is a Jacobean sculpture unique in Ulster. Constructed in marble and alabaster, it has the effigy of Sir Arthur Chichester facing that of his wife, Letitia, while between them is depicted their only child, Arthur, who died young. Below them is an effigy of Sir John Chichester, who was killed at the Battle of Altfracken in 1597 (see chapter 6).

The Chichester Memorial is one of the most sophisticated pieces of Jacobean carving in Ireland. It is almost certainly the work of an English mason.

Sir John Chichester

The Medieval font in the baptistery

One of the wooden screens at the entrance to the Chichester Aisle

The Chichester Memorial

It was probably produced in sections and shipped over to Carrickfergus. The important Chichester family does have other 17th-century memorials in the Church of All Saints', Eggesford, on their Devonshire estate.

The first occupant of the new vault in Carrickfergus was the wife of Sir Arthur Chichester, Letitia, who died on November 27th 1620 and was interred on January 10th 1621. Chichester, himself, died in London in February 1624 and was interred in St Nicholas' Church on October 24th 1624.

Both Sir Arthur Chichester's son John and his brother John were interred in the Chichester vault in 1625. The historian McSkimin, lists a further 24 interments of various descendents of the Chichester family between 1625 and 1860.

On the wall to the right of the aisle is also a marble tablet commemorating Arthur Chichester, third Earl of Donegall, who was killed fighting in Spain. This transept was closed to the public until 1830, but today is open to all for church services.

The Chichester shield

Details of Sir Arthur Chichester and his wife Letitia

Saint John

Of the original trophies and armour relating to Sir Arthur Chichester that would have hung in the aisle over his tomb, only the wooden Chichester shield (or escutcheon) painted with the Chichester family arms and his surcoat constructed of silk, linen and wool have survived to this day. The original surcoat is in the Ulster Museum, while that on display in the church is a modern replica.

At the corner of the Chichester Aisle and the north wall of the chancel is another Medieval pier [21], the last of the early structural elements visible within the later church.

A second Medieval cross slab [22] is located in an alcove to the left of the entrance in the north chancel wall.

Saint Andrew

Saints Columba, Patrick and Aidan

The Stained Glass Windows

Throughout the church are a number of striking 20th century stained glass windows. These include: *The Good Samaritan*, the *Good Shepherd* and the *Prodigal Son* all by Lady Glenavy (1912). *Saint Andrew* (1929) is by Catherine O'Brien, and *Saints Columba, Patrick* and *Aidan* (1912) and *Saint John* (1929) are both by Ethel Rhind.

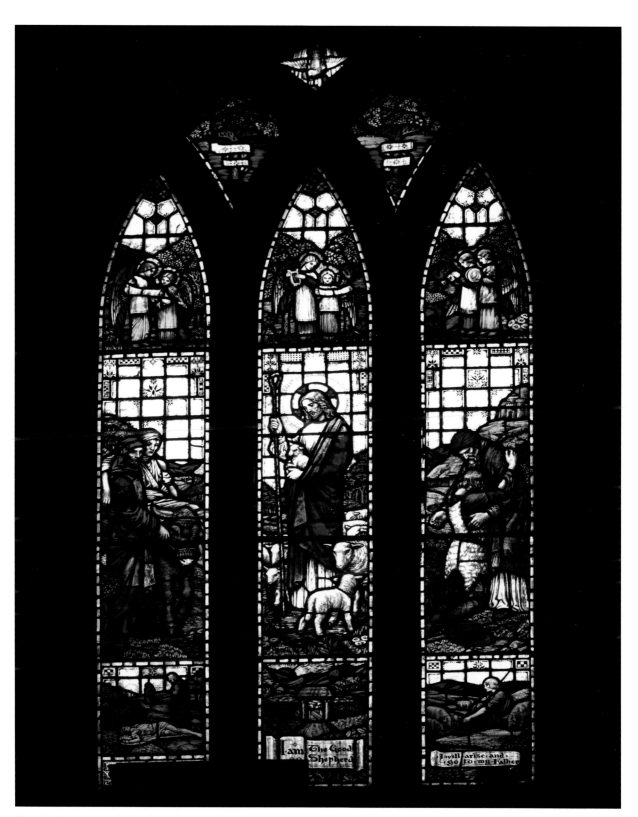

The Good Samaritan, the Good Shepherd and the Prodigal Son

Other Architectural Features

The Spire and Steeple

The original church tower, built over the west porch, had no spire but contained a clock and bell. The clock was put in place in 1678 and had a single hand. The bell was a gift to the parish by Andrew Willoughby, mayor of the borough in 1683. In 1832 this bell was found to be cracked and had to be re-cast in Belfast.

In 1778 the old steeple was taken down and the present steeple and spire erected. A new clock was placed in it,

St Nicholas' Church

together with the bells of the former steeple. In 1932 the tower and spire were renovated.

The War Memorial Bell Tower

This structure, in the church grounds, was completed in 1962 and replaced the old tower, which was in a dangerous condition. It allows entrance to the churchyard at the top of Market Place. The original archway, built in 1831, was retained and incorporated into the new tower.

St Nicholas' Church: Further Reading

Drew, T. (1872) *The Ancient Church of St Nicholas, Carrickfergus, Diocese of Connor: A Report to the Right Rev. Robert Knox, D.D., Lord Bishop of Down and Connor and Dromore,* Belfast (W. Erskine Mayne) and Dublin (E. Ponsonby)

McAuley, T. (no date given) *Parish of Carrickfergus Saint Nicholas' Church: A view of St Nicholas' Church as I see it,* Carrickfergus (privately published)

McConnell, C. (1999) *The Family of Chichester and Carrickfergus,* Carrickfergus (Carrickfergus Borough Council)

McNeill, T.E. (1980) *Anglo-Norman Ulster,* Edinburgh (John Donald)

McSkimin, S. (1909) *The History and Antiquities of the County of the Town of Carrickfergus.* Belfast (3rd edn by E. McCrum of the 1812 original)

Mitchell, Rev. G.A. (1962) *A Guide to Saint Nicholas' Church Carrickfergus,* Carrickfergus. (privately published)

St Nicholas' Church, Carrickfergus
www.saintnicholas.org.uk/

The War Memorial bell tower

Sir Arthur Chichester

9. Carrickfergus in the 17th Century

The Town Under Sir Arthur Chichester

Sir Arthur Chichester arrived in Carrickfergus in the autumn of 1599 to take command of the garrison. He was born in May 1563, the second son of Sir John and Lady Gertrude Chichester whose country seat was Rawleigh Manor, near Barnstaple in Devon. He had a chequered early career, which gave rise to stories of highway robbery and flight from England. After a period of time spent 'on the run' in Ireland, he was eventually pardoned and given command of a ship during the period of threat of Spanish invasion in the late 1580s. He was given a captaincy and fought in Portugal, the West Indies and Puerto Rico alongside Sir Francis Drake from 1589 to 1596.

Thereafter he fought in France, where he was knighted by the French king, Henry IV, before coming to Ireland where he was initially based in Drogheda. Here he was given command of a regiment under the second Earl of Essex.

For much of the Nine Years War things had gone well for the Gaelic Irish. There had been victories at Clontibret in May 1595, the Yellow Ford in August 1598 and the Moyry Pass in October 1601. However, the type of mobile warfare that the Gaelic forces preferred could not, on its own, force the English out of Ireland. What was needed was an outright victory in a major pitched battle.

Hugh O'Neill, sometimes known as the the 'Great O'Neill' by the Irish, and the Earl of Tyrone by the English, was principal Gaelic leader in this war. He realised that Spanish troops would probably be needed to bring things to a conclusion and requests were sent for military aid. As the war dragged on, the English forces were invigorated by the appointment in February 1600 of a new commander, Charles Blount, better known as the Lord Deputy Mountjoy. He initially concentrated his efforts on subduing Leinster and south Ulster. At the same time, two of his commanders, Sir George Carew in Munster and Sir Henry Docwra in the newly fortified post of Derry, opened new fronts against Hugh O'Neill and the Gaelic alliance. The tide of the war was turning.

As part of the new strategy, in August 1600 Sir Arthur Chichester was ordered by Mountjoy to lay complete waste to the Gaelic territories within 20 miles of Carrickfergus, and further afield if possible. This was to be a real 'scorched earth' policy in which every person and all property was a potential target. From his letters, it would seem that Chichester had few qualms about carrying out his orders. In one account he describes how he:

'The Great O'Neill'

Charles Blount, Lord Mountjoy

… burned along the lough [Lough Neagh] within four miles of Dungannon and killed one hundred people, sparing none, of what quality, age or sex so ever, besides many burned to death; we kill man, woman and child; horse, beast and whosoever we find.

In another he elaborates on his views of this type of total war, affirming that:

I have often said and written it is famine which must consume them [the Gaelic Irish and Scots]; our swords and other endeavours work not that speedie effect which is expected.

For the Gaelic allies things were getting desperate. Their only hope lay in the aid from the Spanish Crown sought by O'Neill. Spanish troops finally arrived in September 1601 off the coast of County Cork, and entrenched themselves at Kinsale. Mountjoy's English army put the town under siege while the Gaelic armies of Ulster, led by Hugh O'Neill and Red Hugh O'Donnell marched the length of Ireland to assist them. The decisive battle of the war was fought on December 24th 1601, with the Irish and Spanish being utterly defeated. Much to Chichester's displeasure, however, Hugh O'Neill survived capture in Ulster before finally negotiating his surrender to Mountjoy in March 1603 (the Treaty of Mellifont) and bringing the Nine Years War to a close.

Although he was pardoned, the position of O'Neill and the other rebellious Gaelic chiefs in Ulster became untenable, as they were regarded with complete suspicion by the Crown. On September 4th 1607, Hugh O'Neill, Earl of Tyrone, Rory O'Donnell, Earl of Tyrconnell (Donegal), Cúconnacht Maguire, Lord of Fermanagh and about 100 followers left for Spain by boat

The Irish at war

from the port of Rathmullan in County Donegal in an episode known now as the Flight of the Earls. They hoped to return to Ireland with further Spanish military aid but never did.

The Walled Town

During the last years of the Nine Years War, as events went more favourably for the English forces in Ireland, Carrickfergus was not put under direct threat of attack and its defences were not tested. As described in previous chapters, during the Late-Medieval Period the citizens of Carrickfergus had three lines of town defence — the earthworks, the individual tower houses and, as a last resort, the castle.

It was only at the close of the Nine Years War, and with Sir Arthur Chichester in residence, that the town got the substantial defences for which the townspeople had so long appealed. In April 1599, Chichester had been appointed Governor of Carrickfergus and in February 1605, he became Lord Deputy of Ireland. Amongst the estates awarded to him after the Nine Years War were lands in Counties Donegal, Down and Antrim (including the town of Belfast). Between 1608 and 1615, under Chichester's direction,

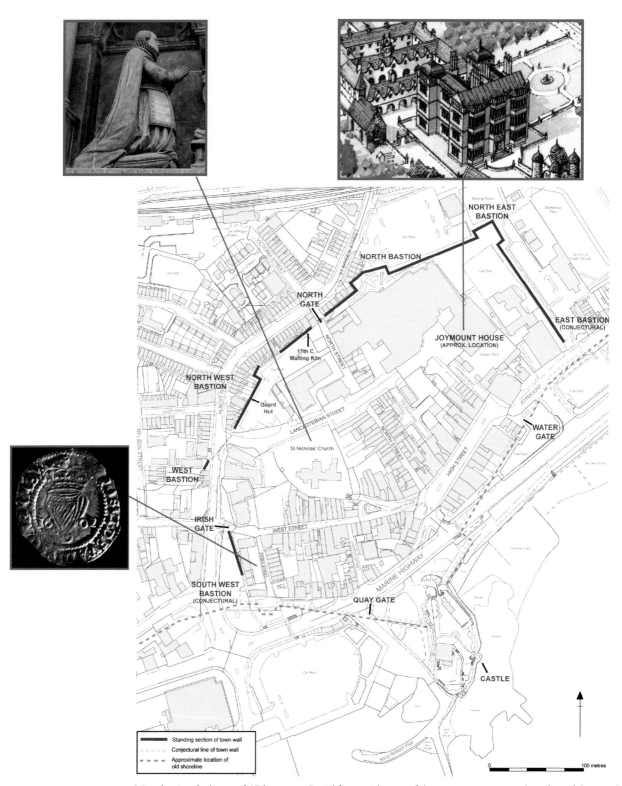

Map showing the layout of 17th-century Carrickfergus with some of the main monuments and artefacts of the period

Carrickfergus was entirely walled in stone, enclosing some 11 hectares. His own large dwelling, Joymount House, was constructed at the eastern side of the town, and the area surrounding the house subsequently became known as Joymount.

Roughly one half, or 600 metres, of the early 17th-century town wall currently survives above ground level, on average 2 metres thick and 3–5 metres high to the top, which is battlemented. The town walls are described in more detail in the next section of the book.

Joymount House

Construction of Joymount House began in 1610 and was completed in 1618. Unfortunately the building was demolished in 1768, and the only depiction we have of it, which appears to show it as a masterpiece of Jacobean architecture, survives as an inset to Thomas Phillips' 1685 map of the town. However, several contemporary descriptions do survive. In 1635, Sir

Joymount House redrawn from the 1685 map

William Brereton described it as a '... verye statelye house, or rather like a prince's pallace...', going on to say that it had:

> ... a verye faire hall and a stately staircase, and a faire dineing roome, carrying the proportion of the hall... the windowes and roomes and

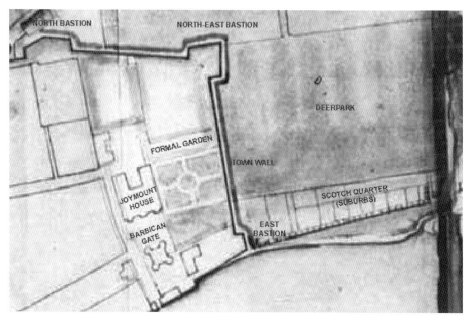

Detail of Joymount House and gardens from Thomas Phillips' 1685 map

whole frame of the house is over large and vast; and in this house may you observe the inconvenience of great buildings, which require an unreasonable charge to keep them in repaire, soe they are a burthen to the owners of them.

The gardens at Joymount House were also described by Brereton as:

Fine Gardens and mighty spatious Orchards and they say they beare goode store of Fruite. I observed on either side of this garden, there is a Dovehouse placed, one opposite to the other in the corner of the garden, and twixt the garden and the Orchards, a most convenient place for apricockes, or some such tender Fruite, to be planted against the Dovehouse wall, that by the advantage of the heat thereof, they may be rendered more fruit-full and come sooner to maturitie, but this use is not made thereof.

Brereton also noted that '… almost all the houses in this town were built castle-wise …', while in 1666, de Rocheford described Joymount House as:

… a great pavilion having … I think, as many windows are there are days in the year; the top is turreted and defended with balustrades, the entry is handsome.

As late as 1708, the writer Molyneux described Joymount House as:

… extremely great and noble, but wanting the gardens of Belfast, which, were they joined, would make beyond comparison the finest improvement in Ireland.

Some archaeological excavation has occurred at the site of Joymount House. In 1949 and 1950, Martyn Jope investigated the early 17th-century town walls at Joymount. In his account of the excavations he stated that:

… the one piece of walling encountered near the street front of Joymount, running towards the sea, was probably part of Chichester's house. It is surprising that no greater remains of this one-time magnificent house were encountered.

Nine pieces of pottery were recovered from under the town wall, sealed between it and the old ground level on which it was built. Most of these were Medieval, but two were Post-Medieval, '… as was in current use in England during the later 16th and first half of the 17th centuries'. It is unfortunate that no detailed description of the Joymount House wall, location plan, or photographs accompanied the published report.

In the summary of excavations carried out by Tom Delaney in the area of Carrickfergus named after the house (Joymount) it states that:

The base of the surviving tower from the Joymount Barbican

... the area excavated corresponded approximately with the gardens of Joymount in the late 17th century. Only its seaward end had been built on in the 19th century, and this building was demolished in 1972 to make way for a local authority development. During its demolition fragments of window mullions and jambs were found built into the walls, and three pieces of oak were removed and dendro-dated to 1559 + 9, 1605 + 9, and 1622 + 9. Both stone and timber would appear to have been originally used in Chichester's Joymount House.

One of the towers of the Barbican within the Joymount complex, has possibly survived, attached to the east wall of the current town Hall. It may have been retained as a watch tower after Joymount House was demolished

The base of the 17th-century O'Neill Chalice showing the Latin inscription and date

and this has protected it from destruction.

The Restoration of St Nicholas' Church

Chichester directed the restoration of St Nicholas' Church in 1614, and stone tablets commemorating the work still survive in the church. Amongst the parts of the church restored was the nave, within which he constructed a private chapel and barrel vault where family members were to be buried. He died in London on February 19th 1624, and in October 1624 was buried in the Chichester vault in St Nicholas'.

The O'Neill Chalice

The 17th-century gilt-silver O'Neill Chalice from Carrickfergus

Although the religious order had been suppressed by Elizabeth I in the mid-16th century, a residence for the Franciscans was re-established in the district of Carrickfergus in 1626. Fr Edmond [Mac] Cana was appointed its new Superior. An extraordinary and beautiful religious artefact survives from this period, the O'Neill Chalice, which dates from 1632. It is made of gilt-silver

Reconstruction drawing of Carrickfergus, in 1620

Imported Portuguese pottery, mid-17th century

and bears the inscription *F. Paulus O'Neill caraud pro Conventu Carfergus fieri 1632*. Fr Paul O'Neill (listed in Franciscan records as being elected Superior on August 15th 1629) was responsible for making the chalice on behalf of the monastery of Carrickfergus in 1632. The chalice is still used in services by the congregation of St Nicholas' in Minorca Place, Carrickfergus, to this day.

Growing Prosperity

In a description by Richard Dobbs of Carrickfergus in 1683, he observed that buildings within the town were '… general built of limestone or brick, and slate house.' and Thomas Phillips' map of 1685 seems to portray Carrickfergus at its most prosperous. The town is shown fully walled, with defences linked to the castle and harbour. The plan of Joymount House, gardens and possible deer park are clearly indicated. Perhaps most interesting is the portrayal of the growth of suburbs, both immediately to the east (Scotch Quarter) and west (Irish Quarter) of the walled town. Scotch Quarter was established by Scottish

Sir Phelim O'Neill

immigrants from Argyll and Galloway, while Irish Quarter grew up as a result of a 1678 decree banning Catholics from all corporate towns and forts. The inset drawing on Phillips' map also portrays the stone buildings and walls of the town, Joymount House, the thatched cottages of Scotch Quarter along the shore and Carrickfergus Castle.

The prosperity of the town in the mid-17th century seems to be borne out by the fact that in 1637 the custom receipts at Carrickfergus (which also included dues collected at Belfast) ranked second amongst Ulster ports to those at Londonderry. However, in reality this figure probably reflects more on the growing economic success of Belfast than it does upon the state of Carrickfergus.

The 1641 Rising

In October 1641, the descendants of the dispossessed Gaelic families led by Sir Phelim O'Neill, and their followers rebelled and attacked plantation settlements all over Ulster (the 1641 Rising). As in the Nine Years

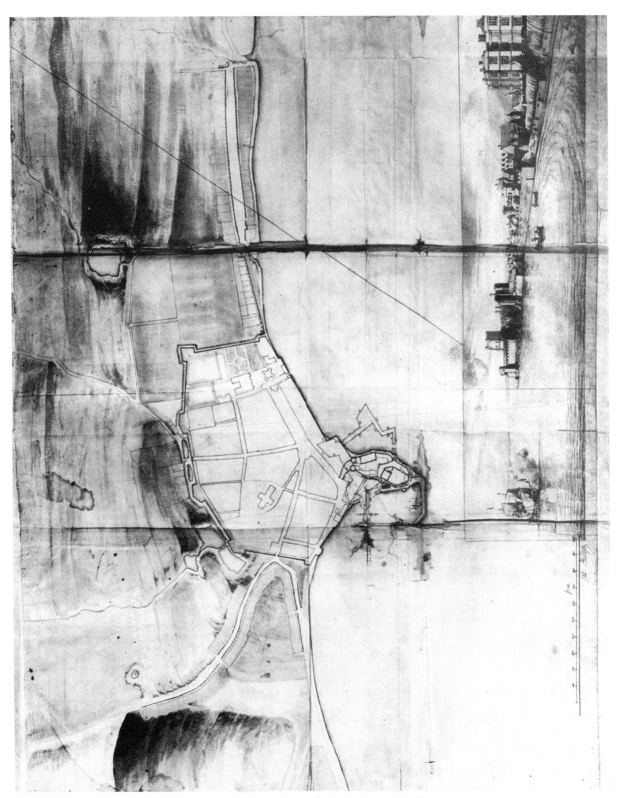

Map of Carrickfergus in 1685 by Thomas Phillips (National Library of Ireland, MS 3137 (42))

General Frederick Schomberg

King William III

War, the Irish rarely had the capacity to attack fortified towns, so these became safe havens for the Protestant settlers. Such was the case with Carrickfergus, where the Governor of the town was Colonel Arthur Chichester, nephew of Sir Arthur Chichester.

There followed a general uprising of Catholics all over Ireland leading to a decade of warfare which has become known as The Confederate War, 1641–53. This conflict was also linked with the civil wars in Britain (1642–51) and the whole decade is sometimes described as The War of the Three Kingdoms. In a confusing melee of engagements there were combinations of Irish, English, Scottish Covenanter, Royalist and Parliamentarian armies in action at various times in Ireland. Commanders and forces sometimes changed sides, and peace was not enforced until the string of victories won by the Cromwellian generals Ireton, Coote and Ludlow that brought the war to a close in 1653.

In April 1642, Major General Robert Monro and an army of 3,000 Scottish troops landed in Carrickfergus to help deal with 1641 Rising in Ulster. Colonel Arthur Chichester withdrew with his regiment to Belfast and the English Parliament made General Monro the Commander-in-Chief of the English and Scottish troops in Ulster. From 1642 to 1648, the Scottish army in Ulster operated mostly independently of the Crown, being opposed to both the Irish Catholics and the Royalists of King Charles II. With the changing allegiances of the Scottish Presbyterians and their new alliance to Charles II (in return for a promise of freedom of religion) in 1646, Munro and his troops declared loyalty to the King. However, in September 1648 a surprise attack on Carrickfergus by a Parliamentary force under Sir Robert Adair led to the capture of the town without a fight and the

departure to England of Robert Monro as a prisoner. In June 1649, Carrickfergus changed hands again when a Royalist force under General George Munro, nephew of General Robert Munro, captured it after a short siege. A few months later, the town changed hands for the last time during these wars when the parliamentary general Colonel Robert Venables captured Carrickfergus after another short siege. Colonel Venables was then made Governor of the town.

Mutiny and Siege

In May 1666, after having not been paid for three months, the garrison of Carrickfergus, consisting of four companies of troops, mutinied and the rebellious troops seized the town and castle. The insurrection was forcibly put down by the Earl of Arran. Nine of the mutineers were hung and the rest transported to the West Indies. As result there were no troops available, nor money to pay them, to guard the town or castle. To remedy this, in July 1666 the Lord Lieutenant of Ireland, the Duke of Ormond, authorised the mayor of Carrickfergus to raise a Militia Company.

During the Williamite War (1689–1691) a Jacobite garrison held Carrickfergus town and castle, though the townspeople were overwhelmingly Williamite. On August 20th 1689, the Williamite General Frederick Schomberg put the town under siege. After seven days of bombardment the town and castle fell. Several breaches were made in the town wall, with the one to the east of the North Gate, between the north and north-east bastions still visible today, despite having been repaired afterwards.

With a landing place secured, King William III landed in Ireland at Carrickfergus on June 14th 1690. The

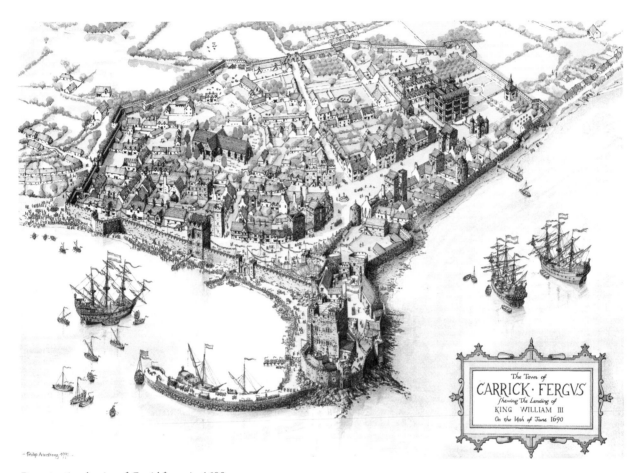

Reconstruction drawing of Carrickfergus in 1690

war was to last another year before he emerged victorious, but Carrickfergus saw no further action.

Finds from Excavations in Carrickfergus

Excavations carried out by the author at Essex Street in 1992 uncovered the stone remains of a substantial rectangular building, butting onto the town wall and situated close to the West/Irish Gate. From its internal layout and the types of artefacts recovered, this structure has been interpreted as a barracks built in the second half of the 17th century and demolished and infilled in the more peaceful 18th

The Medieval and Tudor town ditches at Essex Street

A 17th-century building excavated at Essex Street

North Devon sgraffito ware pottery. This type of pottery is commonly found on 17th-century sites in Ulster

The flue and chamber of a 17th-century malting kiln in the town wall beside the North Gate

century. Evidence of small-scale manufacturing has also been uncovered within the town. Close to the North Gate, and built into the town wall, is a kiln chamber and flue. Excavation, again carried out in 1992 by the author, adjacent to the kiln uncovered the remains of walls and many 17th-century artefacts. It seems certain that this was the location of a malting kiln dating from 1684, listed in Carrickfergus Corporation records, but thought to have been destroyed.

The large quantity of artefacts recovered from the various excavations in Carrickfergus, and their quality, gives a picture of Carrickfergus in the 17th century as a very prosperous port and town. Pottery was imported from France, Spain, Italy, Portugal and Germany. Exploiting the Chichester family connection with England, there were also large quantities of Devon and Staffordshire pottery brought into Ireland.

The population of the town must have grown steadily during the 17th century. The census of 1659 notes 596 adults.

More than 100 Late-Elizabethan base-copper pennies and halfpennies, dated to either 1601 or 1602, were recovered from excavations in the town. Some were in such good condition that the dates and legend were clearly visible when they were uncovered.

Finds of a more personal nature included dress pins of various sizes and types, buttons, leather shoes, fine drinking glasses and fragments of textile. Lead cloth seals attest to fine materials being brought into the town. The greater availability of cheaper tobacco from the colonies is reflected in the large numbers of clay pipes imported from London, Bristol, Rainford and even Holland, and also by clay pipes made in Carrickfergus.

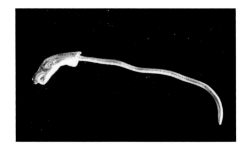

The gold hair pin found during excavations at Essex Street in 1992

Perhaps the most beautiful artefact uncovered from the recent excavations was a small, gold, woman's hair pin, only five centimetres long, with one end shaped as the head of an animal. This exquisite piece of jewellery was probably made in Spain.

But the fortunes of Carrickfergus were changing again. Perhaps the defining date in its Post-Medieval history is 1728, the year in which Chichester's descendents left Carrickfergus for permanent residence in Belfast.

Late-Elizabethan pennies and halfpennies found during excavations in Essex Street in 1991–92

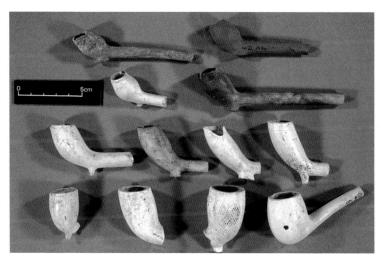

Clay pipes found in Carrickfergus. In chronological order from top left, first half of the 17th century, to bottom right, circa 1900. The orange pipe (top right) was probably made in Carrickfergus using local clay.

10. A Walk Through 17th-century Carrickfergus

A visitor to late 17th-century Carrickfergus would have found the town almost unrecognisable from that of the late 16th century. Firstly, the town had slightly expanded in area and was now completely surrounded by a substantial stone wall. Moreover, the eastern side of the town, where once the Franciscan Friary and later the 'Pallace' had stood, was now occupied by a magnificent Jacobean house and gardens. St Nicholas' Church, so long in disrepair, was now restored and was once again the parish church of Carrickfergus.

Within the town, the visitor would have noted that the buildings were now mostly of stone. Whether the beehive houses still existed is uncertain as, unfortunately, the map of 1685 shows only the principal buildings of the town. It is likely, however, that the poorer Irish and Scots now lived in the thatched cottages portrayed immediately adjacent and outside the town walls.

Undoubtedly the visitor would have encountered many soldiers in the town, since for much of the century there would have been significant numbers of soldiers either based in, or passing through, Carrickfergus to take part in the various wars that plagued 17th-century Ireland. A Williamite cannonball, on display in St Nicholas' Church, is one of the reminders of this period of the turbulent history of the town.

Nevertheless, the visitor would have been most impressed by the dynamic, social settlement that Carrickfergus had become. Descriptions of the 17th-century town and the vast quantity of excavated quality artefacts show that Carrickfergus

Dated ceramic tile from the town

was at its most prosperous during this period. It was the county town, the centre of political, administrative, military and economic power in Ulster. With the Chichester family in residence, it was also the centre of social life in the region. The town was clearly a thriving port, and the same seas that brought the soldiers to the wars also brought in highly-prized commodities from all over Europe to be bought or sold on by its citizens.

11. Focus on the 17th-century Town Walls of Carrickfergus

The walls at Carrickfergus are the oldest stone town walls in Ulster and are some of the best preserved historic town walls in the whole of Ireland. The historic core of Carrickfergus from the early 17th century onwards is the area now bounded by the largely surviving 17th-century town walls that enclose the following streets: High Street, West Street, Lancasterian Street, Antrim Street, Cheston Street, Castle Street and Essex Street. Most of the surviving walls are a State Care Monument, entered into the NISMR as Antrim 052:061, and some sections of the wall are also Scheduled. Since the 1980s the Environment and Heritage Service: Built Heritage has carried out sympathetic conservation works on the surviving wall fabric.

The modern visitor to Carrickfergus will experience a different sort of town than has existed for most of its long history. The essential and symbiotic relationship that existed for centuries between the town and the castle was severed by the construction of a major road, the Marine Highway (now re-named the Causeway Coastal Route), in the 1960s and the altered townscape can sometimes be difficult to understand.

Description of the Walls

About half, or approximately 600 metres, of the 17th-century town wall still survives above ground today. It does not seem to have been built on a plinth, except where it adjoined with bastions. The 17th-century construction included a wall walkway, with access gained to this by steps in the wall (still extant at Joymount and Lancasterian Street). Most of the fabric of the walls consists of local basalt with sandstone being brought in from further up the Antrim coast for the quoins and other dressed elements. In their original form, the landward circuit of the walls consisted of four bastions and two gates giving entry into the town. Along the shoreline there were two half-bastions and two gates, and these fortifications linked up with defensive works at the entrance to the castle, so that the town was doubly defended.

There is a good description, recorded by Benn (1877, 674–75), from the report of the Plantation Commissioners in 1611 of the works that Chichester commissioned for the new town defences:

At Knockfargus we found many masons and labourers at work about the erection and building of the walls of that town and sundry quarry men and labourers at work about a quarter of a mile from the town in breaking of rough stones for the works…4 ox teams [and] 2 horse teams and many garrons [for] drawing of stones and of other materials, 4 lime kilns on fire employed in burning of limestone for the same. And we were advised…that there are 2

The north-east bastion at Joymount

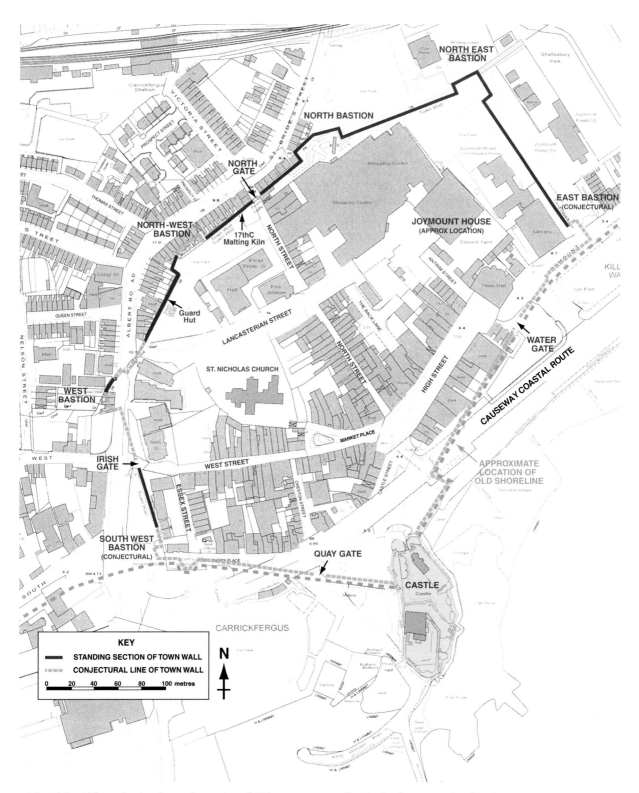

Map of Carrickfergus showing the standing sections of 17th-century town wall and other features mentioned in the text

quarrymen with other labourers employed continually in breaking of limestone about 3 miles away…at Whitehead… and 4 masons with other labourers about 40 miles away [at Cushendun] in breaking and scaffolding freestones for coynes for the bulwarks and to face the wall 6 foot high all along the S part of the town by the seaside, wherein we find that great quantity of freestone must be employed which is got with much difficulty because the boats cannot come near the [quarry place] …the work of the said walls and bulwarks already done contain in length 120 perches [2520 feet/ 756m]…the foundation doth contain in thickness 8 foot [2.4m] … 4 foot deep [1.2m] and in some places 6 and 7 foot deep [2m] and in 20 perches [126m] thereof, at least where the mill streams and uneven ground and highways have been, are 16 foot [4.8m] deep and in some places more. The height of so much of the wall as is now built from the ground, is in some places 7 foot and in other 8 foot and the thickness of the wall throughout is 5 foot [1.5m] …a boat of 8 tons…and a barge of 15 tons which was purposely made for that work…and continually employed in bringing limestone, freestone and other materials…good store of coal ready provided for burning lime.

The best-preserved stretch is at Joymount and facing Shaftesbury Park, along with the north and north-east bastions. The walls are built of large basalt stones in very distinct courses; the larger stones in the lower courses give added stability.

A low red brick wall running at right angles to the north-eastern bastion contains a considerable quantity of hand-made brick. The wall corresponds with one portrayed on the 1685 Phillips' map and appears to delineate an extra-mural deer park, part of the recreation grounds connected to Joymount House. That this 17th-century red brick wall still survives is another remarkable example of the level of preservation at Carrickfergus.

In 1641, the strength of the town walls protected Carrickfergus from possible attack during the 1641 Rising. However, in August 1689 during the siege by the Williamite general, Frederick Schomberg, the walls were

The town wall and north-east bastion at Joymount

The 17th-century red brick wall at Joymount

The inside of north-east bastion

Detail

Detail

The guard hut in the town wall at the western end of Lancasterian Street

breached at various points, most notably close to the North Gate and to the east of it. In 1760, when the French admiral Commodore François Thurot made a surprise attack on the town, the walls were breached near Joymount, at the south-eastern corner of the circuit, close to the old shoreline. Archaeological excavation of several of the bastions during the 1970s and 1990s proved that they had never been properly supported by clay infill, as was the usual case in conventional European military architecture. There is no good explanation for this. The clay would have buffered the bastions against incoming cannon balls and would have enabled cannon to be mounted within them for the defence of the town.

The town defences, laid out with angle bastions, were specifically designed as artillery fortifications, for use of ordnance and also for defence against it. This contrasts with the earlier layout, which conformed to pre-gunpowder military architecture. The stone bastions were not properly rampiered, as the slightly later walls of Derry were, but the form is classic and is in line with the style of building of fortifications, both in earth and stone,

practised throughout Ireland from the late 1580s onwards.

A guard hut built of stone, with later repairs of red brick, is located at the western end of Lancasterian Street and opposite St Nicholas' Church. It was accessed from steps built into the wall. This guard hut blocks access further along the wall, which implies that the town wall was divided up into defensive segments, perhaps allocated to distinct groups of soldiers or citizen militia.

A large stretch of the town wall was demolished in the 18th century to enable Carrickfergus to expand south-westwards (towards Belfast), although its line – and the 17th-century West or Irish Gate – was uncovered during the excavations of the 1970s.

By 1821, three of the gates – Irish Gate, Quay Gate and the Water Gate – had been demolished. When Governor's Place was connected to Irish

Quarter South in 1838, the two half-bastions at the south-western corner and adjoining walls were removed. The final major damage to the 17th-century town walls was caused between 1851 and 1856 by the construction of Albert Road, which removed above-ground evidence for the section between Irish Gate and Lancasterian Street.

The best-preserved of the entrances into Carrickfergus, the North Gate, was heavily altered in the 19th and early 20th centuries. A small arch was created for pedestrians between 1840 and 1850, and the original masonry above the arch was replaced with cut stone in 1911 to mark the accession of George V.

The 19th and 20th centuries saw Carrickfergus in economic decline, with

The foundations of the 17th-century Irish or West Gate into Carrickfergus and the large stretch of 17th-century town wall uncovered during the excavations of 1976–78. In the background is Delaney Green and the Tom Delaney monument, erected in memory of the archaeologist who did so much to uncover and promote the history and archaeology of Carrickfergus. Some repairs were made to the town walls and gates in 1715, at the time of the perceived threat from James Stewart, the 'Old Pretender'.

Black and white photograph of the North Gate looking into town, pre-renovation of 1911

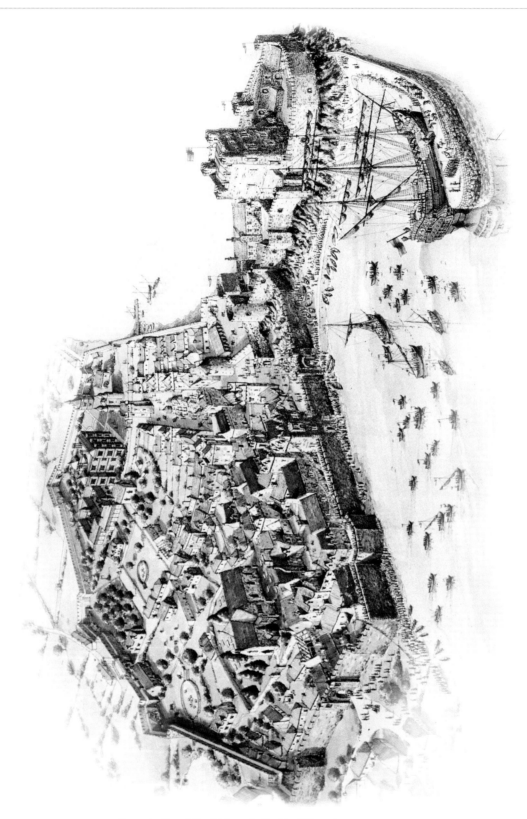

Reconstruction of Carrickfergus in the late 17th century

little substantial development for nearly 200 years. It remained the county town until the mid-19th century, but the town grew little, resulting in the preservation of much of its Medieval and Post-Medieval archaeology. Major redevelopment schemes started in the late 1960s with the building of the Marine Highway along the Antrim Coast and ushered in the era of modern archaeological excavations within the town.

Despite the loss of some stretches of the historic town wall, enough of the monument survives to give the modern visitor to Carrickfergus the feeling of what it must have been like to live within a walled town 400 years ago. Most of the town wall still survives above ground, but this important monument and cultural asset is often eclipsed by the presence of the nearby and better known castle. The survival of such an impressive urban fortification is to be celebrated as an important cultural asset, and Carrickfergus rightly takes its place amongst the most celebrated of walled historic towns in Ireland.

Carrickfergus is part of the Irish Walled Towns Network along with 18 other towns across Ireland, and is one of the two northern towns – the other being Derry – where substantial historic walls remain. The Irish Walled Towns Network is formally linked to the Walled Town Friendship Circle, which promotes the sustainable development of walled towns, castles and fortified historic towns across Europe. Notable members include Carcassone (France), Chester (England) and Dubrovnik (Croatia).

Carrickfergus Town Walls: Further Reading

Ó Baoill, R. (1993) 'Recent excavations in Medieval Carrickfergus', *Carrickfergus and District Historical Journal*, 7, 54–63

— (1998) 'Further excavations in Medieval Carrickfergus', *Carrickfergus and District Historical Journal*, 9, 25–32

— (2007) 'Carrickfergus, Co. Antrim: a walled town in the seventeenth century', *Archaeology Ireland Heritage Guide*, 36

Robinson, P. (1986) *Carrickfergus. Irish Historic Towns Atlas*, no. 3, Royal Irish Academy, Dublin

Simpson, M.L. and Dickson, A. (1981) 'Excavations in Carrickfergus, Co. Antrim, 1972–1979', *Medieval Archaeology*, 14, 78–89

Thomas, A. (1992) *The Walled Towns of Ireland*, 2 vols, Dublin (Irish Academic Press)

The Irish Walled Towns Network, www.heritagecouncil.ie/walled_towns/index.html

Tin-glazed earthenware

12. The Later History of Carrickfergus

In the last few centuries, the fortunes of Carrickfergus have declined as a result of the inexorable rise of Belfast. There were signs of this from the mid-17th century, with Belfast trading profits in excess of those of Carrickfergus. However, in an age of war and invasion such as the 17th century, with its strong stone walls and even stronger castle, the town remained the most important settlement in Ulster. Although the Chichesters were granted Belfast, they never saw fit to wall the town in stone, and in the early days the family clearly regarded Carrickfergus as their principal seat, with the family burial place at St Nicholas' Church.

For a while in the late 17th and early 18th centuries the high quality clay found along the Belfast side of Carrickfergus was exploited by Belfast potters to produce delftware (tin-glazed earthenware) in the Belfast Potthouse (pottery) on Waring Street. Pottery had been made in Carrickfergus using local clay from Medieval times onwards, and later clay pipes were manufactured as well. However, the Potthouse was a much more substantial and important enterprise that flourished from around 1697 to about 1725, and meant that Belfast was able to compete on an equal footing with the biggest English potteries (London, Liverpool and Bristol). A variety of types of delftware vessels were produced, many of which have been found on excavations within historic Belfast.

As Ireland became more peaceful from the 18th century onwards, the potential of Belfast became more apparent. It possessed no stone walls to hinder development within the historic core (though its earthen defences did influence the layout of the town). It possessed a deep-water harbour and the town was a vibrant mercantile and manufacturing centre. Finally, it lay on the main route from Dublin, the centre of British administration in Ireland. Although the town walls and gates of Carrickfergus were strengthened in

Painting of Carrickfergus circa 1850 by Anthony Carey Stannus (Lady Mairi Bury)

1715 in fear of the' Old Pretender', the decline of the town continued. In 1724, Chichester's descendents left Carrickfergus for Belfast. Because of its better communications and harbour, Belfast superseded Carrickfergus as the social, economic and administrative centre of the north of Ireland.

Despite this, exciting incidents still punctuated the later history of Carrickfergus.

The French are in the Bay!

During the Seven Years' War (1756–63), France hoped to invade Britain and so break her control of the seas. These ultimately unfulfilled plans involved Carrickfergus in one of the most exciting episodes in her long history. Commodore François Thurot along with three French ships of the line and 600 troops, landed at Kilroot, two miles to the east of the town, on February 21st 1760. Look-outs from the castle spotted the ships and the town was put under alert. A reconnaissance party of soldiers sent from Carrickfergus confirmed the arrival of the French troops, and that an attack on the town was imminent. After disembarking and forming into regiments, the French army advanced from Kilroot along the shore, through the village of Boneybefore and the suburb of Scotch Quarter.

The first main engagement between the French troops and the Carrickfergus garrison, the 62nd Regiment of Foot under the command of Lieutenant Colonel John Jennings, took place at Joymount, close to the south-east bastion and the shore (beside the present public library). The first assault was repulsed, but ammunition began to run low and firing from the defenders became less sustained. The French army was able to storm the walls and break through into the town. The garrison was forced back

initially to the far end of High Street and then, as more French troops entered the town via the North Gate, into the castle.

Although it was the strongest building in Carrickfergus, the castle had been allowed to fall into disrepair, and its principal use was as a detention centre for French prisoners captured during the Seven Years' War. When Thurot's forces attacked, there were no cannon mounted on the walls and a 15-metre long collapse of masonry in the south curtain wall that had occurred in 1754 had not been repaired. There was also a shortage of ammunition that meant sustained firing could not be kept up. Buttons from the men's uniforms were fired from the muskets in addition to lead shot. A desperate battle took place as the French tried to storm the castle gates, and in hand-to-hand fighting the French troops were initially driven back. But soon after, Colonel Jennings, realising that the position of the garrison was untenable, was forced to sue for terms.

The victorious French troops, now in possession of Carrickfergus, allowed very generous surrender terms for the 197 officers and men. They were permitted to march out of the castle with their arms and colours, and to return to their barracks on parole as prisoners of war. In the several hours of the battle to take Carrickfergus, four men from the garrison were killed and twelve wounded, while the French lost some 19 with another 30 wounded. The French dead were buried on land close to the castle, but it is uncertain exactly where.

The French army spent six days in Carrrickfergus refitting and gathering supplies. As Carrickfergus did not have sufficient stocks, a request was sent to Belfast along with a threat to burn both Carrickfergus and Belfast if these were not furnished. The supplies duly arrived and the French troops embarked on February 26th. Two days later, off the

Commodore François Thurot

French soldiers

An 18th-century cannon

Isle of Man, they were intercepted by a squadron of ships from the Royal Navy, and in a brisk battle the French ships were overcome and captured. Amongst the casualties of the battle was Thurot, who was buried with full honours on the island.

The following map was published in *British Magazine* in May 1760, several months after the French occupation of Carrickfergus. Several of the letters in the accompanying key refer to the episodes of the battle:

C Gateways and passages forced by the Enemy [the French]

H The Old Breach [the wall in the castle which had collapsed in 1754 and had not been repaired at the time the French attacked]

K An old ruinous Wall under Cover of which the Enemy [the French] marched to attack the Castle.

Also of note is the depiction of Lord Donnegall's House and Gardens (B in the map key). In 1768, just eight years after the map was drawn up, Joymount House was demolished.

A site at Kilroot, where the French landed, is still known as Thurot's Well (NISMR Antrim 053:006) and so the dramatic events are now immortalised in the landscape and folklore of County Antrim.

The move of the Chichesters from Carrickfergus to Belfast and their obvious preference for that settlement was indicative of the continued decline that

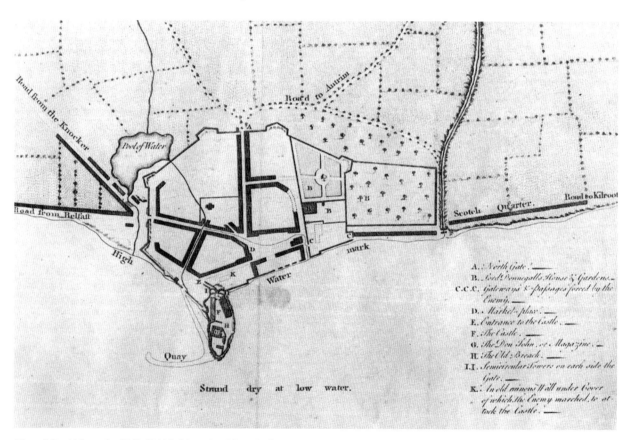

Map of Carrickfergus in 1760 (British Magazine, May 1760)

Victorian shipyards in Carrickfergus

Carrickfergus was undergoing. In 1779, the site of the former Jacobean mansion, Joymount, was given to the Corporation for the construction of a new County Antrim courthouse and gaol.

The Americans are in the Bay!

Less than 20 years after the French captured Carrickfergus, another dramatic military episode occurred. During the American Revolution, the fledgling United States did not have a proper, standing navy. However, some enterprising captains acted as privateers and harassed British ships wherever they were able to find them. These privateers often worked with the assistance of the French, either operating from French ports or in ships loaned by the French. One such enterprising captain was Paul Jones, and on April 24th 1778 this American privateer, in his ship the Ranger attacked the Royal Navy frigate the Drake, moored in Carrickfergus Bay. The battle lasted over an hour and the Americans were successful. Captain Jones then sailed to the French port of Brest with the Drake as his prize.

Victorian Carrickfergus

In 1842, the first Presbyterian Assembly took place in Carrickfergus (possibly held in St Nicholas' Church). Carrickfergus remained the county town until the mid-19th century, but the town grew little.

Shipbuilding in Carrickfergus

In the mid to late-19th century, shipbuilding was carried on at Carrickfergus. The need for vessels to export mined salt and goods made locally, as well as for importing coal, helped the industry to expand. In 1841 there were only three shipwrights operating at Carrickfergus, while a decade later there were twenty-three. The first vessel, a brigantine called the David Legg, was completed in 1845 by Bowman, Logan and Company. Other notable shipwrights operating out of Carrickfergus were Robert Johnston, his son-in-law Paul Rogers and John Hilditch.

were stationed in Belfast and Carrickfergus, between July 1848 and 1849. Jellalabad commemorates their survival of a six-month siege in the town of that name during the first Afghan war of 1841–42.

An interesting glimpse of Carrickfergus' history in more peaceful times is given in the Regimental History of the period (kindly supplied by Brigadier Alastair Fyfe, Regimental Secretary (Somerset), in a letter dated April 28th 1993). After an inspection of the Regiment on October 1st 1849 it was recommended:

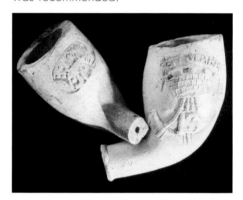

19th-century clay pipes. The 'Jellalabad' bowl is on the right

Victorian view of High Street

Two very interesting Victorian artefacts were discovered from excavations in Lancasterian Street in 1992. The first was a medal commemorating the opening of the new harbour at Carrickfergus (now the East/Albert Edward and West/Alexandria piers) by the Prince and Princess of Wales on April 27th 1885. The second was an elaborately decorated clay pipe bowl with a military motif in relief and the name 'Jellalabad' prominently displayed. This pipe dates from the mid-19th century when Prince Albert's Regiment of Light Infantry (now the Somerset Light Infantry)

...that a change of quarters would be desirable, the men seem to have got too intimate with the women both at Belfast and Carrickfergus. Women have been known to carry off soldiers from Carrickfergus in a car; taking them to Belfast and keeping them there for several days. There is a good deal of absence from tattoo and staying out at nights.

Carrickfergus Gasworks

Commercial production of coal-gas was introduced to Ireland by the 1820s. By 1899 there were in excess of 100 gasworks in Ulster. Most were public utilities, serving towns and villages, and some were private concerns, supplying mills, workers'

Commemorative medal

houses and those of the rich. Opened in 1855, Carrickfergus Gasworks supplied the town with gas until 1965, and was closed in 1987. The gasworks used coal-burning furnaces to fuel the street lamps of the town and surrounding area and to provide gas for cooking. The gasworks contains Europe's largest surviving set of horizontal retorts, mini-furnaces in which the gas was made by baking (rather than burning) coal. The gas was piped around the region after purification. Each of the retorts had two stokers, one of whom packed the coal into the furnace, while the other removed the coke.

The Carrickfergus Gasworks was a successful business, and in 1900 it produced 4 million cubic feet of gas, supplying 172 customers. By 1913 this had risen to 8.5 million cubic feet and 580 consumers, and in 1943 production was 19 million cubic feet. By 1947 the gasworks included three rooms of retorts containing five benches of 36 horizontal retorts, as well as a diverse range of ancillary structures. These included housing for purification apparatus, exhausters, station meters, governor and a 200,000 cubic foot gasholder. There were three teams of stokers, and the gasworks had a staff of 17. Unfortunately, by the early 1960s, even though 49.3 million cubic feet of gas was being produced for roughly 2,000 customers, the cost of workers' wages and the rising price of coal, and cheaper and more plentiful sources of oil, meant that coal gas had become uneconomic. The coal gas industry was almost obsolete.

Carrickfergus Gasworks, located in Irish Quarter West, is now the only surviving coal gasworks in Ireland and is one of only three left in Ireland or Britain. It is fully intact with buildings and plant dating from 1855 to 1965. It has been completely restored as Flame, the Gasworks Museum of Ireland, and

Carrickfergus Gasworks

was re-opened as a visitor and educational attraction in August 2002. The museum also contains an exhibition of gas appliances dating back to the 19th century.

Gasworks retorts

World War II

During World War II, the basements of the keep of Carrickfergus Castle were used as air-raid shelters. Also during the war, the elite force now known as the US Rangers was formed by volunteers from other American regiments stationed in the north of Ireland who assembled at Sunnylands, Carrickfergus. The new 1st Ranger Battalion, under the command of Major William O. Darby, was formed on June 19th 1942.

The Modern Town

It was not until the mid-20th century that substantial redevelopment began to take place again in Carrickfergus. There was reclamation of land around the castle and harbour, obscuring the old coastline, and the construction of the major new coast road through the town, the Marine Highway. Now that the town is separated from the castle by a busy four-lane road, visitors unacquainted with the town's long history, cannot appreciate the fact that the town and castle were previously a single unit. This is unfortunate, because the nature and context of Carrickfergus have now been radically altered. Perhaps at some future date the coast road will be realigned and the castle and town re-united as of old.

In 2004 a new Carrickfergus Museum and Civic Centre was opened at 11 Antrim Street, in the town centre. The Museum contains a selection of artefacts from archaeological excavations carried out within the town, as well as suits of armour from the Elizabethan Period onwards. The exhibitions are a mixture of audio-visual and interactive displays. Amongst the interesting exhibits are a collection of 28 of the finest atlas maps from the period 1690–1720. These were given as a present by King Louis XIV to Richard Kane of Carrickfergus, who was on his way to taking up the position of military governor of the island of Minorca.

The fact that there was little significant development within the historic nucleus of the town from the mid-17th century until the mid-20th century means that the many layers of history which accumulated over the centuries have survived and can be investigated by archaeologists. In some cases, the remains of buildings that are hundreds of years old, were uncovered just centimetres below the modern ground-surface of the town. The archaeological excavations that have taken place over the last few decades have told us much about life in Carrickfergus over the last 800 years. There is still much to learn and future excavations will undoubtedly increase our knowledge about this most historic and important town.

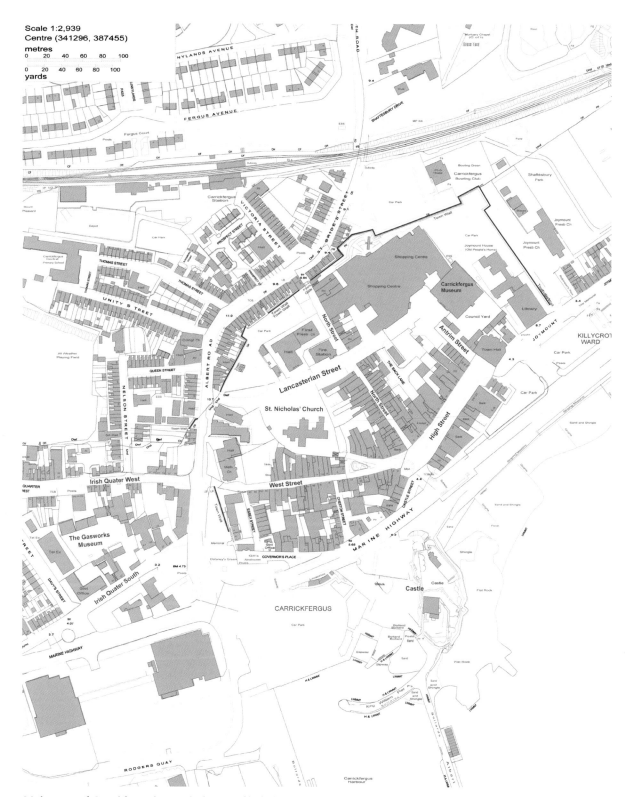

Modern map of Carrickfergus showing the location of both the Carrickfergus Gasworks and Carrickfergus Museum

Aerial view of Carrickfergus in 2008, showing important features of the Town

A Later History: Further Reading

Beresford, M. (1972) 'François Thurot and the French attack on Carrickfergus 1759-60', *The Irish Sword*, 10 (1971–72), 255–274

Campbell, G. and Gunn-King, B.J. May, (1980) *Historic Buildings, Groups of Buildings, Areas of Architectural Importance in the town of Carrickfergus*, Belfast (Ulster Architectural Heritage Society) revised edn of publication prepared between November 1975 and April 1978 by Gordon Campbell and Susan Crowther

Francis, P. (1994) 'The Belfast Potthouse, Carrickfergus clay and the spread of the delftware industry', *Transactions English Ceramic Circle*, 15, part 2, 267–282

Francis, P. (1992) 'The fine-ceramic potteries of Belfast and the Carrickfergus clay trade', unpublished MA thesis (Queen's University Belfast)

Hammond, F. (1989) 'Like a phoenix from the flames: Carrickfergus Gasworks', *Carrickfergus and District Historical Journal*, 4 (1988–1989), 23–40

Aerial view of town in 2008

Kennedy, D. (1964) 'Thurot's landing at Carrickfergus', *The Irish Sword*, 6, 1963–64, 149–153

McConnell, C. (1995) *The French are Landing! The forgotten invasion of Carrickfergus in 1760*, Carrickfergus (Carrickfergus Publications)

McSkimin, S. (1909) *The History and Antiquities of the County of the Town of Carrickfergus*, Belfast (3rd edition by E. McCrum of the 1812 original)

Robinson, P. (1986) *Carrickfergus: Irish Historic Towns Atlas*, no. 3, Dublin (Royal Irish Academy)

Carrickfergus: A Select Bibliography

Anon. (1989) 'Carrickfergus visited in 1635 by Sir William Brereton, Bart', *Carrickfergus and District Historical Journal*, 4, 11–16 [The article contains extracts relating to Carrickfergus and Belfast from Brereton's accounts of his travels in mainland Europe, Britain and Ireland.]

Beresford, M. (1972) 'François Thurot and the French attack on Carrickfergus 1759-60', *The Irish Sword*, 10 (1971–72), 255–274

Bigger, F.G. (1909) 'The Franciscan friary at Carrig-Fergus', *Ulster Journal of Archaeology*, 15, 49–60

— (1910) 'Notes on Carrickfergus', *Ulster Journal of Archaeology*, 16, 96

— and Fennell, W.J. (1908) 'The round church of Carrig-Fergus castle', *Ulster Journal of Archaeology*, 14 , 183–189

Brannon, N.F. (1986) 'Carrickfergus' in Hamlin, A. and Lynn, C. (eds) (1988) *Pieces of the Past: Archaeological Excavations by the Department of the Environment for Northern Ireland 1970–1986*, Belfast (HMSO)

Campbell, G. and Gunn-King, B.J. (May, 1980) *Historic Buildings, Groups of Buildings, Areas of Architectural Importance in the town of Carrickfergus*, Belfast (Ulster Architectural Heritage Society) revised edition of publication prepared between November 1975 and April 1978 by Gordon Campbell and Susan Crowther

Crickard, E. (1987) 'Knobbler is coming', *Carrickfergus and District Historical Journal*, 3, 13–15

Donnelly, C.J., Ó Néill, J., McNeill, T.E and McCooey, P. (2005) 'De Courcy's castle: New insights into the first phase of Anglo-Norman building activity at Carrickfergus castle, County Antrim', *Medieval Archaeology*, 49, 311–317

Drew, T. (1872) *The Ancient Church of St Nicholas, Carrickfergus, Diocese of Connor: A Report to the Right Rev. Robert Knox, D.D., Lord Bishop of Down and Connor and Dromore*, Belfast (W. Erskine Mayne) and Dublin (E. Ponsonby)

Duffy, S. (1995) 'The first Ulster plantation: John de Courcy and the Men of Cumbria', in Barry, T., Frame, R. and Simms, K. (eds) (1995) *Colony and Frontier in Medieval Ireland: Essays Presented to J.F. Lydon*, London (The Hambledon Press), 1–27

Francis, P. (1994) 'The Belfast Potthouse, Carrickfergus clay and the spread of the delftware industry', *Transactions English Ceramic Circle*, 15: 2, 267–282

Francis, P. (1992) 'The fine-ceramic potteries of Belfast and the Carrickfergus clay trade', unpublished MA thesis (Queen's University Belfast)

Hammond, F. (1989) 'Like a phoenix from the flames: Carrickfergus Gasworks', *Carrickfergus and District Historical Journal*, 4 (1988–1989), 23–40

Jope, E. M. (1950) 'Excavations in Carrickfergus, 1949–1950', *Ulster Journal of Archaeology*, 13, 61–65

Kennedy, D. (1964) 'Thurot's landing at Carrickfergus', *The Irish Sword*, 6 (1963–64), 149–153

McAuley, T. (no date given) *Parish of Carrickfergus Saint Nicholas' Church: A view of St Nicholas' Church as I see it*, Carrickfergus, (privately published)

MacNeice, J.F. (1928) *Carrickfergus and its contacts*, Belfast (W. Erskine Mayne)

McCavitt, J. (1998) *Sir Arthur Chichester, Lord Deputy of Ireland 1605–16* (Institute of Irish Studies, Queen's University Belfast)

McConnell, C. (1994) *Carrickfergus, A Stroll through Time*, Carrickfergus (Carrickfergus Publications)

— (1995) *The French are Landing! The forgotten invasion of Carrickfergus in 1760*, Carrickfergus (Carrickfergus Publications)

— (1999) *The Family of Chichester and Carrickfergus*, Carrrickfergus (Carrickfergus Borough Council)

— (2002a) *Ramparts: The Defences of Carrickfergus*, Carrickfergus (Carmac Books)

— (2002b) *Tales From the Castle Gate: Carrickfergus Castle*, Carrickfergus (Carmac Books)

McNeill, T.E. (1981) *Carrickfergus Castle*, Belfast (HMSO)

— (1983) 'The Premonstratensian houses of Carrickfergus, White Abbey and Woodburn', *Perita*, 2, 265–266

McSkimin, S. (1909) *The History and Antiquities of the County of the Town of Carrickfergus*, Belfast (3rd edn by E. McCrum of the 1812 original)

Mitchell, Rev. G.A. (1962) *A Guide to Saint Nicholas' Church Carrickfergus*, Carrickfergus, (privately published)

Murphy, E. and Ó Baoill, R. (2000) 'It's a dog's life: Butchered medieval dogs from Carrickfergus, Co. Antrim', *Archaeology Ireland*, 14:51, 24–25

— Ó Baoill, R. and Brannon, N.F. (1998) 'A curious old wall… An unusual horn-core structure from Carrickfergus, Co. Antrim', *Archaeology Ireland*, 12:2, 1998, 16–17

Ó Baoill, R. (1993) 'Recent excavations in Medieval Carrickfergus', *Carrickfergus and District Historical Journal*, 7, 54–63

— (1998) 'Further excavations in Medieval Carrickfergus', *Carrickfergus and District Historical Journal*, 9, 25–32

— (2007a) 'Carrickfergus, Co. Antrim: a walled town in the seventeenth century', *Archaeology Ireland Heritage Guide*, 36

— (2007b) *Guide to Carrickfergus Castle*, Belfast, (Environment and Heritage Service: Built Heritage)

– (2007c) 'The archaeology of post-Medieval Carrickfergus and Belfast, 1550–1750' in Horning, A., Ó Baoill, R., Donnelly, C. and Logue, P, *The Archaeology of Post-Medieval Ireland, circa 1550–circa 1850*, Bray (Wordwell)

– (2008) 'The urban archaeology of Belfast: a review of the evidence', *Ulster Journal of Archaeology*, 65, 8–19.

Pinkerton, W. (1859) 'The "Pallace" of Carrickfergus', *Ulster Journal of Archaeology*, I, 1–10

Robinson, P.S. (1986) *Carrickfergus: Irish Historic Towns Atlas*, no. 3, Dublin (Royal Irish Academy)

Roebuck, P. (1979) 'The making of an Ulster great estate: the Chichesters, barons of Belfast and viscounts of Carrickfergus', *Proceedings of the Royal Irish Academy*, 79C, 1–25

St Nicholas' Church, Carrickfergus **www.saintnicholas.org.uk/**

Simpson, M.L. and Dickson, A. (1981) 'Excavations in Carrickfergus, Co. Antrim, 1972–1979', *Medieval Archaeology*, 25, 78–89

Simpson. M.L., Bryan, P.S., Delaney, T.G. and Dickson, A.I. (1979) 'An early 13th century double-flued pottery kiln at Carrickfergus, Co. Antrim: An interim report', *Medieval Ceramics*, 3, 41–51

Waterman, D.M. (1952) 'Excavations at the entrance to Carrickfergus Castle, 1950', *Ulster Journal of Archaeology*, 15, 103–118

Young, R.M. (1893) 'Notes on the ancient records of Carrickfergus, 1574-1723', *Journal of the Royal Society of Antiquaries of Ireland*, 23, 64–68

Select General Bibliography

Anon. (1855) 'Sir Henry Sidney's memoir of his Government of Ireland', *Ulster Journal of Archaeology*, 3, 33–52, 85–99, 336–357

Black, E. and Maguire, W.A. (eds) (1990) Kings in Conflict: *Ireland in the 1690s*, Belfast (exhibition catalogue, Ulster Museum)

Brady, C. and Gillespie, R. (eds) (1985) *Natives and Newcomers: Essays on the Making of Irish Colonial Society 1534–1641*, Dublin (Irish Academic Press)

Doherty, R. (1998) *The Williamite War in Ireland*, Dublin (Four Courts Press)

Dobbs, R. (1683) 'A brief description of county Antrim, 1683', in Hill, G. (1873) *An Historical Account of the MacDonnells of Antrim*, Belfast (Archer & Sons)

Falls, C. (1950) *Elizabeth's Irish Wars*, London (Methuen & Co.)

Francis, P. (2000) *Irish Delftware, an Illustrated History*, London (Jonathan Horne Publications)

Gillespie, R. (1985) *Colonial Ulster. The Settlement of East Ulster 1600–1641*, Cork (Cork University Press)

Hill, M. (1993) *Fire and Sword: Sorley Boy MacDonnell and the Rise of Clan Ian Mór, 1538–90* London (The Athlone Press)

Horning, A., Ó Baoill, R., Donnelly, C. and Logue, P. (2007) *The Archaeology of Post-Medieval Ireland, circa 1550–circa 1850*, Bray (Wordwell)

Kerrigan, P. M. (1995) *Castles and Fortifications in Ireland 1485–1945*, Cork (Collins Press)

Lenihan, P. (2001) *Confederate Catholics at War 1641–49*, Cork (Cork University Press)

Mac Cuarta, B. SJ (ed.) (1993) *Ulster 1641: Aspects of the Rising*, Belfast (Institute of Irish Studies, The Queen's University of Belfast)

McCavitt, J. (2002) *The Flight of the Earls*, Dublin (Gill and Macmillan)

McGurk, J. (1997) *The Elizabethan Conquest of Ireland*, Manchester (Manchester University Press)

McNeill, T.E. (1980) *Anglo-Norman Ulster*, Edinburgh (John Donald)

Maguire, W.A. (ed.) (1990) *Kings in Conflict: The Revolutionary War in Ireland and its Aftermath 1689–1750*, Belfast (The Blackstaff Press)

Mallory, J.P. and McNeill, T.E. (1991) *The Archaeology of Ulster: From Colonization to Plantation*, Belfast (Institute of Irish Studies, Queen's University of Belfast)

Morgan, H. (1993) *Tyrone's Rebellion*, Dublin (Gill and Macmillan)

Ó Ciardha, É. (2004) *Ireland and the Jacobite Cause, 1685–1766*, Dublin (2nd edn, Four Courts Press)

O'Neill, T. (1987) *Merchants and Mariners in Medieval Ireland*, Dublin (Irish Academic Press)

Thomas, A. (1992) *The Walled Towns of Ireland*, 2 vols, Dublin (Irish Academic Press)

Index

Compiled by Julitta Clancy

Note: references in *italics* denote illustrations